Perfect Your Legering

Ron Lees

The Crowood Press

First Published in 1993 by
The Crowood Press Ltd
Ramsbury, Marlborough
Wiltshire SN8 2HR

British Library Cataloguing-in-Publication Data

A catalogue record for this book is available from the British Library.

ISBN 1 85223 749 X

Throughout this book, the pronouns 'he' and 'his' refer to both men and women.

Acknowledgements

It takes more than just a writer to produce a book. In this case it took the imaginative skills of my good friend Ray Sheppard who supplied some of the reference drawings, my dear daughter-in-law Michelle who contributed in like manner, and I must not forget the kind assistance of Drennan International for their advice on technical matters. Dave Hartle of Droitwich Fishing Tackle was also very kind in supplying material for photographic purposes. To these I offer my heartfelt thanks.

Above all, any dedication must go to my wife Jean. Throughout our years together she has suffered the loony antics of my angling. Though she knows little of fishing, her wise motivation and sound Mancunian advice in 'cutting out the waffle' has been invaluable; without it, this book would never have reached the bookshelves.

I cannot make any particular acknowledgements of literature from which I have taken reference. Over a lifetime an angler will read too many books to list and, in consequence, perhaps any angling book is a subconscious compilation of others. Yet, I firmly believe that an angler must have an 'edge' – the all-important individuality; writers, perhaps, are of similar ilk.

Photo Acknowledgements
Photograph on page 101 appears courtesy of David Halls *Coarse Fishing* Magazine.

Designed by D & N Publishing
The Old Surgery
Crowle Road
Lambourn Berkshire RG16 7NR

Imagesetting by FIDO Imagesetting, Witney, Oxfordshire.

Printed in Great Britain by
Redwood Books, Trowbridge, Wiltshire

Contents

Introduction

Time was when to leger was to be idle. No fisherman sat contemplating a rod end all day, when he could be working – watching the red tip of a float creeping downstream, mending line, or trotting, drop fishing and the like. To leger was the last, lazy method to employ when all was lost, a thing to do for ten minutes while the angler packed away his tackle. Such was the popular school of thought in the 1950s. Isn't it strange how the wheel of knowledge turns...

I cannot remember when I didn't fish. As a product of suburban Birmingham, perhaps it was natural to seek the delights of the countryside, for it is a fact that the vast majority of anglers come from large cities; the paradox is that very few riverside dwellers bother to fish.

At eight years old I lay on the side of a concrete yachting pool in Bournville, near the city centre, catching redbreast sticklebacks as they choked down my small worms. A few years later I poached a lake belonging to the Cadbury family, catching good bream and roach, and it was on this delightful lake that I learned just how effective legering can be.

Two things constantly caused problems. Beside an old broken-down boathouse the lake was fifteen feet deep, much too deep to fish with my ten-foot cane rod and plastic float, while out in the centre, large fish constantly crashed upon the surface, too far away to be reached. With the aid of a coffin lead, however, I legered for the bream beside the boathouse, catching many on paste or maggots. After stripping yards of line from the reel, letting it lie on the grass, I cast way out to those carp with ease, even hooking a few, though landing only one.

In later years, sitting on the banks of the Severn one cold afternoon in the autumn of 1960, the lesson was driven home again. After float fishing for chub for many biteless hours I rested the rod, taking out a flask of hot coffee. As the float settled over the shallow water, the rod almost went off the rest as a fish pulled, breaking the hooklength. On a re-cast the same thing happened. Taking off the float, I cast the terminal tackle into the margin, just a pair of AA shot holding. With this most basic of legering techniques I caught ten pounds of barbel, not one reaching a pound. As a direct result of those two instances, I never again underestimated the value of a bait fished on the bottom. On the majority of occasions it will be the more productive method, especially when angling for specimen fish.

Those were good years for my young soul – important early years which set the pattern for the future, a future which developed into the terminally unsuccessful search for secrets in the catching of fish.

My angling travels have taken me to many countries, meeting fellow anglers from all walks of life and social levels, folk who have one thing in common: that wonderful outlook on life with which a fisherman is blessed;

5

INTRODUCTION

such people are at peace with themselves and this fast world in which we live.

But our gentle art of angling needs forethought. People who are successful, whether at business, sports or in the armed forces, have one thing in common: they plan. They seek out the best sources of information, leaving, as far as is possible, nothing to chance. Such people also have a wide vision, dreaming of their perfect world and how to attain it.

In the case of the angler, if he dreams as I do, he will be underwater with his beloved fish. He will be watching loose maggots fall through the water, wary of the one which falls faster with the weight of the hook. He will imagine groundbait dropping through the clear water amid waving strands of green weed, be alarmed by the soft thread of nylon glinting in the spears of sunlight.

To catch fish in a dream is not too difficult. The beginner to the sport, however, dream as he may, requires basic information which is available from many sources: from tackle shops, where the proprieter is invariably a practising fisherman, the ever-increasing number of forums which take place countrywide, angling videos, idle chatter on river or lakeside, weekly angling publications – and a vast number of books. Many of these books are written for the specialist, from tench to carp, from roach to barbel, while others explain fishing from sea to stream. Although wonderfully written and a delight to read, some books are sadly out of date, for the pace at which tackle improves, and at which specialized methods are developed, is very difficult to keep up with.

The leger angler is a specialist in his own right. The fact that he angles on the bottom, in a manner which requires much imagination, needs perhaps even more careful planning if he is to be successful. If the planning is good, and the application correct, the rewards can be high; but should the approach and application be lackadaisical, he can fall flat on his face.

I have strived in this book to describe legering methods that make it less difficult – and perhaps more pleasant – to catch fish, methods which have been proven over many years by myself and far more successful anglers. Included also are new techniques which have resulted in many a fine net of fish, techniques which may seem overcomplicated, but are devised by anglers with but one thought in mind: that of catching more or bigger fish.

I have strived also not to have a war with my dictionary. Angling should be kept a simple sport, and I have attempted to put the whole thing in simple terms, for I must confess some of the technical terms and applications to modern-day fishing are completely beyond me. As time passes, this high-tech. world in which we live produces wonderful advances in tackle design and materials, but sadly, I still cannot tell how to make certain that an angler *will* catch fish.

Angling is quaintly unique in the attraction it has for its devotees, for we are happy with constant failure. But then – if we were so successful at catching fish all of the time, with two-pound roach or fifty-pound carp commonplace, we would surely become bored and take up some other, less predictable pastime.

Herein, no doubt, lies the secret of this soul-consuming sport of ours. We may go fishing for days on end, to arrive home wet, cold, hungry, biteless, perhaps with a severe cold. We then lie awake, already dreaming of the next magical day at the waterside, with a mind full of whys and ifs and buts, forever seeking answers. The truth of the matter is – there are no answers. We can only continue to go fishing, invent new materials, devise new methods, try new baits, and reach for the moon. Hopefully, no one will ever touch it.

Ron Lees
Droitwich 1993

1   Rod and Reel

From the not too distant chuck-it-and-chance-it days, legering is now a devastating method if approached with some thought. Whilst at one time to leger was considered the thing to do when all else failed, it is now the main attack used by a growing number of anglers.

To leger means to fish on or near the bottom – nothing more, and nothing less. A variation is to paternoster, where the bait, anchored to the bottom, is suspended higher in the water. But *how* to fish on or near the bottom, *how* to bring a swim alive, and what is done when bites are not forthcoming is the difference between success and giving it all up through constant failure. Many things are required to become an accomplished leger angler, and a good idea, perhaps, is to start with tackle requirements.

To walk into a fishing-tackle shop must be one of the most pleasant experiences an angler can enjoy. To browse through a range of rods and reels, to select a balanced stick float, to listen and converse with other anglers gives rise to a feeling of well-being peculiar to anglers only. It can, however, become most frustrating, especially when selecting a major cost item such as a rod.

THE ROD

The development and materials used in the manufacture of rods have made gigantic leaps forward. Not all that long ago a man cut a branch from a tree – he had a rod! The first manufactured rod I am aware of was made from greenheart of two or three sections, held together by brass tubes. From this we progressed to bamboo cane, Tonkin cane, split cane, Spanish reed, and the terribly heavy metal tube. Hollow fibreglass rods came on to the market in the 1950s, and what a boon they were. Amazingly light, made in varying diameters to give differing actions; at last an angler could choose a rod for his needs. Glass reigned supreme until the mid-1970s when carbon was introduced to the market. This gave birth to a new era in rod design, where it is not unusual to find a float rod of more than fifteen feet long weighing but a few ounces.

There are now literally hundreds of good-quality rods to choose from, with the vast majority made from carbon fibre, or the derivatives of kevlar and boron. These materials are so slim and light, yet so strong, that the manufacturers must be nearing the ultimate. (Paradoxically, there are stubborn traditionalists who much prefer heavy, slow-action cane rods. I can understand this; a good cane rod has an action all of its own – it has soul.)

A tackle dealer will show you float rods from five to fifteen feet long, costing from as little as a few pounds to a few hundred pounds. He will demonstrate the varying attributes of tip actions, through actions, and the weight differences of fibreglass, carbon, kevlar, boron, and the like. Mention leger rods and out will come a display of toothpicks of less than six feet long, graduating in size to high-tech. quiver-tip rods of more than twelve feet, followed by swimfeeder rods by the dozen, half- or full-butted varieties, seemingly a rod for all occasions. So where, in the midst of the forest of rods found in a good tackle shop, does the angler new to legering begin?

As cost is a personal matter, depending on how fat one's wallet may be, I will not dwell too much on what to pay; suffice to say that the dearest is not necessarily the best. Many rods today are designed by top anglers, and the commission paid to these experts is built into the overall price. Therefore, the chances are that the magnificent tool as recommended by Joe Bloggs may be made from exactly the same blank as a rod costing half as much. Bearing this fact in mind, you will still get what you pay for.

Legering rods can be broken down into classifications, each with a different application:

Quiver Tip

A basic quiver-tip rod is made from a two-piece blank, to which a thinner, more pliable tip is glued into the narrow end of the shortened top joint. The thin tip is supposed to quiver when a bite occurs, and that explanation sums it all up. However, different species

A standard quiver-tip rod in use. The tip is just bent over by the tautness of the line.

and circumstances demand that a different rod be utilized. A twelve-foot monster capable of throwing 4oz of lead from one side of the Severn to the other would be completely useless if used for bream fishing with a hook-length of less than 1lb breaking strain.

A rod to be used for legering with a simple bomb, or using swimfeeders to medium size, will be of around ten feet in length, be able to handle fish from ounces to a few pounds, and will suffice the needs of the everyday 'pleasure' angler – whatever that may mean. The solid glass tip is tapered to almost a point where the final tiny ring is placed. Intermediate rings of the hard chrome variety are whipped in position, and the cork butt is about 25in in length. With this rod, the pleasure angler can, and will, put many a fine fish into a net.

But what of lack of distance when casting, missed bites, hooks pulled out, broken lines, fish running into reed beds, etc. Fishing ability apart, any of these problems can be placed squarely on the unsuitability of the rod. There is no sensible way in which an angler can carry – or purchase for that matter – every quiver-tip rod he would need for every situation he might encounter. Obviously, a happy medium must be reached.

In the good old match days of the 1970s, constantly on the search for increased catches, we made rods to take a variety of tips which we glued into sleeves. These sleeves were of exactly the same diameter, all of which fitted on to the same rod, a two-piece glass rod of around nine feet, with 18in cut off the top joint. Some anglers went as far as building another rod of stiffer action, thus having a combination of six different rods. The tips were different in taper and length, so giving a choice depending on requirements on the day; quite innovative, they were very successful, though with much room for improvement.

And how they have improved. Today, with the help of computers and high-tech. materials, we can purchase a carbon leger rod weighing less than 6oz which arrives with a selection of push-in tips, all perfectly matched to the parent rod, tips engineered to a predetermined test curve, and tapered, being ground to a fraction of a thousandth of an inch. The rod will be between ten and twelve feet long, the longer version comprising three sections, so eliminating the need for a 7ft long holdall which never fits into the car. Rod rings will be of the lined variety made by Seymo of Fuji, using space-age, materials; no matter how much wear and tear this material is subjected to, no matter how much or how hard the line runs over them, these rings simply do not wear out. The butt, made from either high-density cork or Duplon, a nice soft rubbery substance, will be around 22in in length, reducing the possibility of fouling anything behind, such as a close vertical bank or an outgrowing bush.

Thus we have the multi-tip, a rod that will cover most situations an angler will encounter. Small to medium feeders can also be used with this rod, from a cut-down Drennan Feeder-Link, holding six maggots for winter roach, through to an open-end groundbait feeder for bream fishing. It can be used for virtually any legering application, from picking out the tiny pluck of a gudgeon under the rod end, or to register the 'drop back' bite of a long-distance tench. They are all excellent rods – except for that odd job when something else is needed.

This could be a rod built for heavy swim-feeder fishing, or perhaps a wand, a mini-quiver rod sometimes less than eight feet long. Maybe a swingtip rod, the tip no more than a few inches of cane or solid glass attached by a piece of rubber. Perhaps a spring-tip, where a screw-in tip takes the form of a spring, and a bite is registered by the

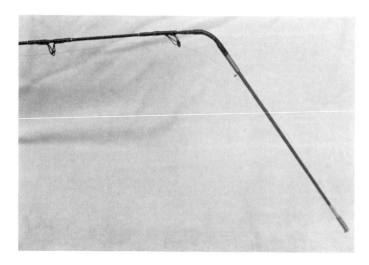

Swing tip in the fishing position. It is important to have some angle to indicate drop-back bites where the tip drops to the perpendicular.

Last, but certainly not least, a situation may call for a 'meat' rod, a form of legering to which I pay special attention in Chapter 5.

Purpose-Built Feeder Rods

The heaviest of feeder rods will chuck a 4oz loaded feeder to more than 80 yards. In casting terms, this is quite a long distance, requiring a rod built to handle strong tackle and strong fish, usually barbel, who attack the feeder and hookbait with enough venom to hook themselves. The rod, therefore, is built with a powerful butt, is of a middle to tip action, with faster than usual taper to arrive at a thin enough tip which will give positive bite indication. The usual length for this type of rod is

break of the spring. Although almost redundant, these still have their devotees, and are covered in more detail in later chapters.

The most powerful legering rod that I know of is used for one simple job, that of catching winter barbel on the lower Severn below Worcester. This grand old river can carry more than six feet of winter floodwater and still be fished, but it needs specialized tackle to do it. The latest development is to use a standard every-day beach-caster, which is supposed to hurl up to 12oz of lead into the river (*see* Chapter 5). Thankfully, it is only a loony fringe of match anglers who use such tackle, with the urge to win overcoming any sense of sport, or indeed even pleasure.

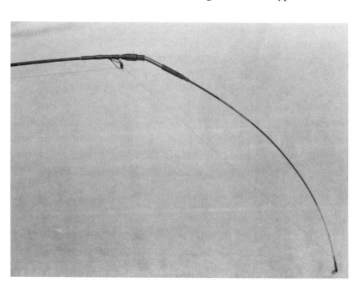

A spring tip 'broken' under pressure. When the tip is pushed completely in it acts as a normal quiver tip.

Modern tip rod with four interchangeable tips of differing diameters.

twelve feet, long enough to hold high in the air, keeping as much line as possible off the water. The extra length also offers the facility of longer, smoother casting, where finer tackle can be considered, and will give better control over big fish. These heavy feeder rods are excellent for the purpose for which they are designed, but not much good for anything else.

A more adaptable rod is the thirteen-foot Drennan Feeder rod which can be purchased with four tips of different thickness and action. This rod has a wide range of applications, from long-distance stillwater bream fishing, to fishing a shallow peg on the far bank of a river at 40 yards, a method which requires as much line as possible to be kept out of the water.

Basic Leger Rod

The leger rod so beloved by anglers of tradition is a simple two-piece rod built from almost any material: cane, fibreglass, with carbon perhaps an unnecessary expense. There are no complicated additions such as tips in any form; the angler either feels for his bites

or watches the movement of line or rod end. Action or length will depend on personal preferences. An experienced fisherman will go through a full range of rods, until the day arrives when he picks up that one certain rod with which he feels comfortable. It may only be for him – but that fisherman will derive so much more pleasure from it.

Wand

The wand is a delicate rod from seven to ten feet in length. It is made from a soft-action leger blank, with the butt cut to within 20in or so of the joint, leaving just enough on which to build the handle. As the use of the wand demands the utmost finesse, the built-in tip must be of the finest proportions, about 15in in length. In the shorter models, where the butt section comprises the whole of the bottom joint, the first ring will be on the upper joint, placed on a section of thin wall. With this rod there is a need to fine everything down, and in respect of rings I would recommend low-profile match rings of the Seymo or Fuji variety.

Used on canals or slow inside swims, the wand is not built to handle big fish. Fine lines to 1lb hooklength can be used with confidence, though it is always wise to fish as heavy as the occasion will allow.

Finish

The colour and finish of a rod may seem unimportant, but a little advice will not, I hope, go amiss. Years ago it was fashionable to matt black everything, including rods. The idea was to prevent things from flashing in the sun, so spooking fish. That was all right and it probably held some truth, but to control a float on a wet matt-blacked rod was nigh on impossible, for the line stuck to the joints. A nice, shiny varnished rod, however, needs only a bang on the butt to remove most of the offending wetness, after which line runs off quite amicably.

It is perhaps wise to use rods that carry some colour, or at least find a rod bag which 'glows'. Apart from looking nice, they can easily be seen in times of gloom, such as tackling down at dusk, following a biteless day in torrential rain. Such a day, when fate shows one of her cruel moods, will be the time to step on a couple of hundred pounds' worth of uninsured rod. A brightly coloured one not only helps to brighten your foul mood, it will be more easily seen!

That just about sums up on rod requirements. A totally dedicated matchman will own many leger rods to do many jobs. When a match is forthcoming he will do his homework and take only the rods he may need. The specimen hunter, too, will own a range of rods, each designed for a particular species, perhaps having three perfectly matched rods for carp fishing, plus pike rods with varying test curves from 1½ to 3lb, and maybe a full range of feeder rods. For general fishing, however, a good thirteen-foot multi-tip feeder rod, a

A corner of the reel room from the collection of R. Coley of Worcestershire.

standard ten-foot medium quiver, and a twelve-foot beast would suffice the needs of most anglers.

THE REEL

In the early, golden days of fishing, the reel was looked upon as little more than an item to contain line – a storehouse, from which line could be taken or returned. In effect, the reel does exactly the same job today, but line is taken in differing ways, returned safer, faster, sometimes even stored in a protective housing.

I remember my first reel with great affection. It was named a 'starback', due to a triple-pointed brass star attached to a spindle set in the centre of the star, on which a shiny hardwood one-piece spool revolved. My father was a gunsmith, and as such could engineer metal to fine tolerances. He took the reel – which groaned when in use and wobbled on the spindle – turning it into a silent work of art, a reel with which one flick of the drum made it spin for nigh on a minute. Though not a high precision centre pin so beloved by Trent anglers, line could still be drawn from the drum by the pull of a river on the float; I quickly learned the delights of trotting, of slowing a float down to present a natural bait. I loved that old reel. It served me for years, catching gudgeon in the local canal at Hopwood near Redditch, roach on the Warwickshire Arrow, chub on the Severn and many more. For legering, however, it was utterly useless.

There are but two main types of reel used in legering: the open- and the closed-face fixed spool. It is a fact that with the open face, longer distances can be achieved with nothing to hinder line movement; the line in a closed-face type comes from within a shrouded housing, thus causing a certain amount of drag. Most anglers, therefore, use the open face for legering.

Though we British are renowned for our leadership in invention and engineering, twentieth-century economics demand that reels are purchased from the Far East. And what nice reels they are. A top-of-the-range open-face reel made from carbon for lightness will be blessed with a coned spool for long-distance casting, rear drag adjustment for control over a running fish, ball bearings for quietness and longevity, a handle which will be ambidextrous, a fast changeable spool,

The ancient and the new. Centre foreground is the ABU 507 – the matchman's favourite.

internal bale-arm action, a retrieve ratio between three or six to one – all of which go to make as perfect a line store as we can devise. The most important feature is perhaps the material used in the bail-arm pick-up point. When chrome was the only hard-faced surface available, the abrasion caused by line running over this surface under pressure from fish and leger was quite dramatic, rubbing a deep groove which cut the line. Nowadays, the bale-arm contact surface on a good-quality reel is virtually indestructible.

The closed-face variety is normally associated with float fishing. The early designs as marketed by the Abu firm of Sweden (the 500 range) were quickly adopted by match anglers, who found the ease of line control when float fishing much to their liking. Strangely, the 500 range was designed for spinning; these reels are built for hard work and long life, and as such are quite useful for legering. Line of 6lb or so is about the limit this type of reel can handle – anything thicker than this comes off the spool in thick coils, resulting in shorter casting, also leading to tangles. For reasons best known to the manufacturers, the original designs of the 500 range were discontinued at the height of their popularity, and to find one in pristine condition now could set you back £100. Though not ambidextrous, they are available in right- or left-hand-wind models.

Whatever your preference may be, one reel will not do for all jobs. A reel suitable for heavy feeder fishing would be totally out of balance if used with a wand. Once again, the poor old leger angler has to dig into his wallet, for he will require at least three reels for his overall needs.

The pressures put on a reel when retrieving four ounces of leaded swimfeeder across a fast weeded river – possibly with a big fish on the end – will soon destroy one poorly made. When heavy feeder fishing, therefore, a sensible approach is to use a strong reel, preferably of the ball-bearing type, capable of holding a couple of hundred yards of 6lb line. A well-designed reel will have a cross-lay movement, where the line, reeled in under pressure, is layed on to the spool in a manner where it cannot cut into itself; this gives rise to clean casting and no tangles. Not much can go wrong with a sturdy reel of this nature, but a good cleaning after each session will pay dividends.

A smaller open-face is needed for lighter work, a reel which balances to the rod. This should have a sensible retrieve, for the speedy 6:1 ratio type is much too fast for this kind of job, resulting in terminal tackle which spins itself into kinks; a nice easy 3:1 ratio is more sensible.

Reels today are made with a built-in clutch, or drag as it is known. The use of the clutch is a feature which many anglers, matchmen in particular, ignore at their peril. Many anglers tighten the clutch solid – or, in the case of closed-face reels, remove it completely – with the idea being to backwind as a fish runs, relying on speed of mind and wrist to sense the point at which line must be given. Fish don't know this, and they have a nasty habit of suddenly bolting off when it is least expected. My advice is to set the clutch sensibly – you can still backwind if you wish.

The choice of make of reel is personal. With this item, perhaps more than any other, the angler gets what he pays for. In these days of industrial copying, many may look similar but are of varying quality, and the angler should, therefore, be very careful. He must be assured of the availability of spares, also of servicing facilities; in this matter, the larger, more reputable firms offer excellent back-up.

To conclude, a new reel should be treated like a new car. Even the engine of a Rolls Royce, if full of rain, river water, sand, groundbait and long-deceased maggots would not last very long unless cleaned and oiled!

2 Hook, Line and Sinker

LINES

Horses for courses, that's what line selection is all about. If you fish for big fish 40 yards away with a feeder rod in a river full of summer weed, it's not much use having a hook-length of 1lb breaking strain. Six-pound reel line and around 3lb hooklength at the least is nearer the mark. On the other hand, fish for roach with a wand on a canal with such line and you would not get a bite.

At the risk of sticking my neck out, I believe many anglers today fish with lines which are unnecessarily strong. Though there can be no doubt that a 10lb line will land a fish more safely than a 4lb line, the very idea of sport has been removed – the poor old fish has no chance. The problem would be, of course, that the angler would get few bites, if any. Furthermore, choice of rod, distance, species sought, baits, presentation, weight of lead, etc. are all factors which must be considered when deciding on line strength.

In my younger, more pedantic days, I carried a small set of scales in my pocket when out to buy a rod. After setting up the rod, in the tackle shop or out on the pavement, I asked the dealer to attach a reel and line, and to thread the rod as normal. Tying the terminal end of the reel line to the scales, I walked away ten paces or so; then, with the dealer pulling mightily on the butt end, I read the scales. Try as I did, I found it impossible to put a 3lb load on a twelve-foot float rod. With today's designs and materials it is almost silly to consider a load of even 2lb being applied to a similar rod. Thus the question must be addressed: why use lines that are too strong for the rod? Everything suffers, including that all-important balance. An exercise I continue to carry out when buying line is to take a micrometer to the tackle shop. It's quite surprising how much a few yards of line can alter in diameter and therefore breaking strain, and it is well worth the trouble of finding a spool of a regular diameter before purchase.

A wise leger angler could well limit himself to three main reel lines. Six pounds for heavy feeder fishing, 4–6lb for general work, touch legering, meat fishing, etc., down to 2.5lb for straight quiver-tip legering or medium to light feeder use. Anything between these parameters is personal choice, depending on special swims and circumstances. Reel line, it will now be seen, is not too important as long as balance is considered in the tackle set-up.

Brand of line is another matter. There are dozens of brands on the market, all excellent, though somewhat distracting even to an experienced angler. We have monofil, nylon, stretch, superstretch, non-stretch, strong, superstrong, (?) sinking, floating – none of which mean a great deal to an angler who, after a long week at work, simply wants to sit on a bank and angle. (The floating line claim, is, I think, a misnomer. Put lead on any line and it will sink. Grease any line and it will float.)

Over the years I tried most lines as they came on to the market, yet I always reverted to Bayer Perlon, or Drennan Floating line – they are one and the same, manufactured in Germany. It is reliable, thin enough for any given diameter, has excellent knot strength and will not kink; it is also one of the least expensive. (Throughout this book, the breaking strains of lines are taken from the Bayer Perlon scale.) Maxima is also an excellent line, recognized as the best line for legering due to its sinking properties.

Hooklength

There are many more very good lines available, but whatever the angler chooses, there are basic rules to consider, especially in the area of the hooklength. Not many fish feed by wrapping their respective heads around a bait – they suck the bait in, and if a heavy line or hook prevents the bait acting in similar fashion to a loose-feed offering, they will eject it in a flash. Natural presentation of the bait, therefore, must be the aim of every thinking angler; it is a fact that the thinner the line at the hook – assuming the size of hook is balanced to the line and choice of bait – the more readily fish will take the bait. The hooklength, therefore, is of prime importance.

Technology today has produced lines of quite amazing strengths when diameter is considered. Where before a line of 1.7lb b/s would have been 0.12mm thick, a line of similar thickness today is closer to 3lb. So where do we go from here? Should we change to the new 1.7 b/s hooklength, so reducing the thickness and getting more bites, or do we use the same thickness, which means the same results as before with the benefit of using a stronger line? This would depend on the type of swim being fished. If it is snagless, then it

would be daft not to take advantage of the thinner line. A snaggy swim would of course require the thicker line.

Problems with these thin lines are many. Kinking and heat created by line friction, or caused by shot or float movement, will soon reduce the breaking strain. New knots have been developed for these lines, though problems continue to occur; all I can suggest is that when tying a knot, a lick of saliva will provide the necessary lubrication. However, I must point out that no matter which knots are used with this high-tech. line, a knot of any description in any line reduces the breaking strain dramatically. All in all, I do not believe the leger angler has need for such ultra finesse or expense.

Some Popular Knots used in Angling

Blood knot.
A means of tying together two lines of similar or different diameters.
Tucked half blood.
Perhaps the most important of all knots, for the tying on of line to swivel, bead, leger, or anything else where only one line is used.
Water knot.
A simple multi-turn knot used in many situations, including the forming of a loop.
Hook-tie knot.
For tying on hooks, either spade or eyed.
Water loop.
Another method of attaching the lead-link.
Whipping knot.
For applying rod rings.
My own.
Nameless, but a sliding knot which does all I require it to.

Apart from perhaps my own knot, these are the main knots used in fishing. Others have been invented by people of great ingenuity, though few do more than those described.

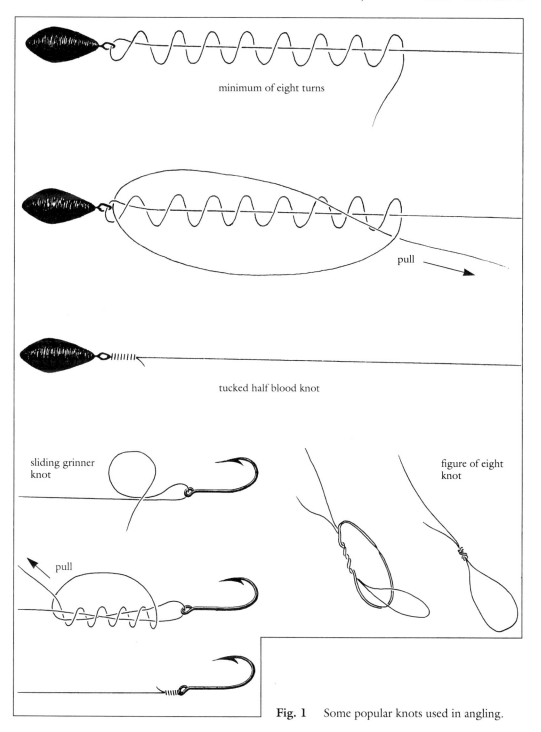

minimum of eight turns

pull

tucked half blood knot

sliding grinner
knot

figure of eight
knot

pull

Fig. 1   Some popular knots used in angling.

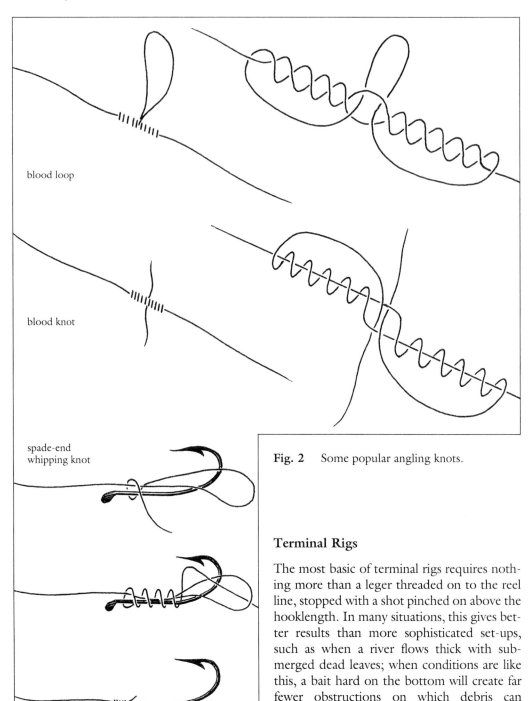

blood loop

blood knot

spade-end
whipping knot

Fig. 2 Some popular angling knots.

Terminal Rigs

The most basic of terminal rigs requires nothing more than a leger threaded on to the reel line, stopped with a shot pinched on above the hooklength. In many situations, this gives better results than more sophisticated set-ups, such as when a river flows thick with submerged dead leaves; when conditions are like this, a bait hard on the bottom will create far fewer obstructions on which debris can become stuck. In more general situations, there is still nothing to compare with a simple link leger which is no more than a lead attached to a separate piece of line, attached in turn to the reel line somewhere above the hook. For most uses a lead-link tied to a water loop is quite adequate, but there are occasions when adjustments must be made over the course of a session where the link must be moveable. In this rig the link is attached with a sliding loop, or a small (balanced) swivel. To prevent this falling down to the hook, a form of stop of one kind or another is required. An item called a leger stop may be purchased: a small bung which fits tight into a tiny tube slipped on to the line. In my experience it doesn't do much more than squash the line – it certainly will not stop a 2oz leger sliding down to the hook.

The attachment of a heavy feeder rig must be well secured. Two swivels are required: one for the running link and one for the attachment of the hooklength. This is a basic set-up, but the terrible tangles experienced when using this method over the years have given birth to some quite innovatives items, many of which are now standard in the kit of a dedicated feederman. Bits of valve rubber to cover swivels are a nice idea, though I'm not so sure about the bits threaded on to the line above whatever form of leger stop is in use. This is to absorb shock when casting; in practice it does nothing. Another idea is to use extra-strong pole elastic for feeder attachment, which on the face of it is good sense, for we have a built-in shock absorber. I only used this once. I almost killed myself.

It was match practice day on the Severn at Arley, a day of sun, ramblers, and canoes; barbel – the quarry – were few and far between. The Severn here changes constantly. Within a hundred yards will be rapids inches deep, followed by a slower stretch which may plunge into an extremely deep hole. The more placid areas are covered almost from bank to bank with green waving beds of ranunculus, flora

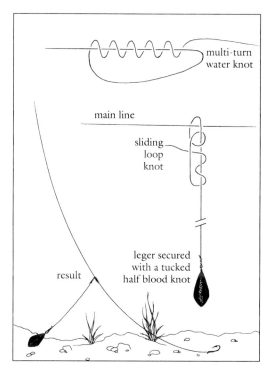

Fig. 3   Basic terminal rig knots.

which grows across the surface no matter how strong the current. In this weed live the barbel, hiding from sight, feeding off the snails and insects which live there, where the only sensible way to fish for them is to plonk a feeder in a slightly deeper channel in between the weeds.

At some time during the day – after missing a few bites which I blamed on the heavy feeder – I tied on the pole elastic feeder link. Eventually the tip rattled to signify a bite, with which I failed to connect, and on the retrieve the feeder stuck solid in the surface weed. Following a tug of war between myself and the offending bank of weed, and with the elastic at full stretch, the lead-loaded feeder, anchored not ten yards away, suddenly came loose, bulleting through the air to hit me smack in the face. Since that day I'm ready to duck at any time when snagged. A 4oz feeder or similar lump of lead can quite feasibly put you – or a bystander – in hospital.

Rigs suitable for 'straight' legering (without a feeder) using say a reel line of 2.5 or so, need nothing other than a lead link attached with a sliding knot, which is stopped by either a multi-turn water knot in the reel line, or a small shot nipped on top of the hooklength knot. Complications on terminal rigs are all too frequent and should be avoided if possible. There are, however, specialized rigs explained in further detail where applicable elsewhere in this book.

HOOKS

These are *the* most important of all the main tackle requirements. An angler can take his pick of the world's tackle, but if his hook isn't right it all counts for nothing. Choice of hook pattern and size are of prime importance when considering different species, and are dealt with in the appropriate place, but a few general hints here will not go amiss.

Any ideas of cost-cutting with hooks must be avoided like the proverbial plague. Many are cheap at about 100 for £1, and are perhaps adequate for holiday anglers who never fish at any other time, but for the serious angler they are simply not up to the job.

The specimen hunter will opt for the eyed variety of hook. When after strong-fighting fish such as carp or barbel, this is perhaps good insurance, for by virtue of its design, the eyed hook is stronger than a spade-end type, though it does have the drawback of being heavier and more bulky. For fish who are choosy – and that includes just about every fish I know of – the choice must be spade-end.

Most anglers tie their own hooks, either at home or on the bankside. The home tier needs to cut line of a predetermined length

and breaking strain, tying a batch which he knows will be of the same length, for when changing a hook, the need for fine adjustments to terminal angles should be minimal. He can whip these by hand, using the hook tie knot, or use a hook-tying machine available from a tackle dealer. For those with fumbling fingers, this little item is easy to use and a great boon, leaving a hook perfectly tied. If, like myself, you prefer to tie a hook direct to the reel line, the same device can be used in the fishing situation.

In my early days of fishing I bought one hook for a penny. The brand name was Superfection, the pattern Model Perfect, and it was made in Redditch. It was a short-shanked round-bend hook, gold coloured, which took maggots, bread, worms, wasp grub, wheat and anything else I thought would catch fish. It was whipped with fine silk to gut and finished with a soft varnish, and was a hook which lasted as long as the line didn't break, sometimes for months on end. These hooks were tied to Luron, one of the first nylon lines.

In the late 1950s and for reasons unknown to me, there was a turn around of allegiance. Despite Redditch being the traditional home of makers of good hooks for years, it was to Mustad of Sweden that we looked for an affordable good selection. The choice of pattern may have had something to do with this act of piscatorial treason, for an angler had at his fingertips models such as forged reversed, flattened, sproat bend, limerick bend, round bend, crystal bend, extra short shank, long shank, extra long shank, thick wire, 3 ex. fine wire, wide gape, blued, silver, black, red – just about any hook any angler would want for any occasion. Barbless hooks, too, were readily available for the conservation minded.

Mustad continue to thrive today, though are looking over their shoulders at the influx of hooks from the Far East – and look hard they must, for these imported hooks are excellent indeed. For those anglers who have reservations regarding barbless hooks (which, for certain species includes myself) whisker and micro barb designs are a great leap forward, not only in the field of conservation, but also in the speed at which hooks can be removed from the mouth of a fish. Italy, too, is making inroads into the market with the Tubertini series, while the Drennan firm also market two excellent ranges of hooks, including Kamasan.

Anglers carry many views about hooks, and to become involved in a discussion will leave you with a headache. The angling world is rife with tales of a hook which may have been a number one choice for years. A period arrives when fish after fish falls off the hook, after which the old favourite is suddenly cast aside, simply because the user lost a few fish. On the face of it one may think this is rather hasty. Perhaps the fish were 'taking short', the rather loose term given to those occasions when it's difficult to connect with a bite, the theory being that the fish simply taste the bait without actually taking it into their mouths.

Practically, to change the hook pattern is sound common sense. In a match situation, or in the search for a specimen, the change of hook in these circumstances becomes a dire necessity, for the angler will have lost confidence in his original pattern. To fish without confidence in any item of tackle, be it rod, reel – and *especially* the hook – is plain stupidity. With his new choice, he will have so much more confidence, and fish better as a result.

One precaution I always make when purchasing a box of hooks is to give a tweak or two to a few points with my fingernail. If they snap off, they are either too brittle or the barb is cut too deep, and should be rejected.

The leger angler need not get too tied up in hook selection. When using big baits for big fish, such as barbel or carp, his choice will be an eyed, forged hook with lasting strength. Chub,

perhaps not quite 'the fearfullest of fish' as described by Walton, have mouths big enough to take in a bait the size of a golf ball, and a strong-eyed hook would be advisable. Certain conditions, however, will require a small bait with a small hook to suit. On hard-fished match or day-ticket waters where chub are treated to gallons of maggots or casters every week, and where every chub in the venue has been hooked a few dozen times, it's not unusual to have to go down to size 22 to get a bite. Most good-class crystal hooks will suffice, a Kamasan B920 being ideal as it is forged from flattened fine wire to give that bit of extra strength.

Roach are more finicky, where success or failure can depend on choice and size of hook.

David Hall with a nice catch of Kennet roach and bream. The one being held weighed 2lb 3oz and fell to a legered maggot.

On most waters I know, a 1lb roach is big, a 2lb fish being a rarity. They are fished for with a range of baits, maggots, casters, hempseed, tares and bread being among the favourites. The perfectionist will use a different hook for each of these baits, the size and even the shape changing with each bait.

Hooks are covered in detail as each species is dealt with, but one inescapable fact remains. Over the years I have always been aware that hooks are very personal. A fisherman will have his favourites and should stick with them.

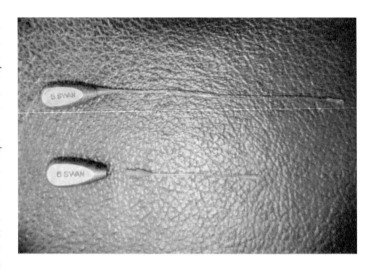

Drennan Leger-Link. The range of leads are all interchangeable by the threaded end of the nylon link.

LEGERS

Types of leger must be considered as certain patterns are used for different styles of legering. The most simple of legers is a split shot, the largest being the SSG, or swan shot, one of which is adequate for legering close under the rod end in still, shallow water. The number of shot can be added to where necessary, though I think more than three can lead to tangles when it is far better to use a small bomb.

The Arlesey bomb as designed by Dick Walker was shaped for distance casting, and though virtually universal in its applications, it is all but useless on a flooded, rushing river. In such conditions, a lead with flat sides is needed, one which cannot roll. On the other hand, a flat coffin lead stuck on the bed of river or lake, will perhaps lie flat and immovable, and is not much good where a twitching technique is employed; in this instance, an Arlesey bomb belted with a hammer to give it flat sides is unbeatable.

The ball leger, or drilled bullet, is a must for the rolling leger technique, and a range of sizes to suit varying conditions should rattle away in the tackle box of every serious angler. When using a ball leger for the first time, it's necessary to smooth the exit holes on either end to remove the possibility of any sharp edge cutting the line.

The Drennan Leger-Link system is a brilliant concept. A flattened bomb-shaped non-toxic leger is threaded on to a 2in length of special nylon which has a hole moulded into the end through which the reel line is threaded. Each lead can be changed at will by simply screwing one off and replacing it with one of a different size, the ideal situation when the river changes pace or the angler wishes to fish at longer distance. The nylon link will stretch to 4in if so desired, giving a further number of computations. The Seymo range of screw-on bottle leads is also excellent.

BITE INDICATORS

The most commonly used bite indicator is the quiver tip. Matchmen and pleasure anglers find this adequate for most situations, using tips of varying thicknesses for stillwater and differing river conditions.

The bobbin-type indicator is a more delicate method, used mainly by specimen hunters, which, in turn, leads to it being a dire neccessity during the hours of darkness. Two rod rests are required, the front one positioned lower than the rear to allow the rod to be pointed at the bait after the cast has been made. In times of stormy conditions, the rests can be positioned where the tip of the rod is below water level, removing the effect of wind.

Following the cast, loose line is taken in and the rod placed in the rests. The most basic form of bobbin is a piece of bread squeezed on to the line between the reel and first ring. A little line is drawn from the reel, where the bobbin will hang down; when a fish takes the bait, it rises, and the resulting strike will shake the bread from the line.

A more advanced idea is to utilize the top of a washing-up liquid container, tying it to a piece of line which is in turn tied to the rod rest. After the line is pulled from the reel, the bottle top is hung over the line below the bottom ring. When it rises, and the strike is made, the top is pulled off due to it being secured to the rod rest. A clothes peg will perform the same function. It is now common practice to see night anglers using a highly visible drop-off indicator of very large proportions, yet extremely light to facilitate the delicacy required.

A butt indicator is clipped to the rod by a built-in clip, and the line is placed under a small 'grab' device. When a bite occurs, the arm of the indicator rises, remaining in this position throughout any consequential playing of a fish. This may seem a cumbersome

This demonstrates how to use a brolly to shield the tip. In this case, a bank stick is used as a bite indicator.

method, but is quite effective, especially in a gale when the water carries high waves.

However, modern angling technology has improved on these methods immeasurably. The most advanced set-up would be to utilize a highly visible 'monkey-climber', a device which slides up a slim metal stick anchored to the ground. This will be adjustable to combat a light current, with a positive line-release mechanism to free the line.

A modern audible bite indicator is virtually computerized. There are various designs available, though the circuitry on the more expensive is so complex that one can cost almost as much as a small television. The device is attached to the top of the front rod rest in the

Clip-on butt indicator. Ideal for windy conditions.

normal fashion, after which the line is placed in the 'V' access. In this slot is a spring-activated mechanism which touches the line. When the line moves – even a fraction – the circuit is made where a micro-speaker emits a 'bleep', while at the same time a small bulb gives further visual warning. The pressure can be adjusted to activate the sound, decided by the conditions such as current, wind, etc. By using these wonderful items, the angler is free to look at bird and bee, to cook his sustenance, even to sleep. But the night angler should also be aware that ducks, bats and birds can, and will, produce the same result.

A number of anglers use both bobbin and optonic in their rigs, for many species. In the chapters which follow, the bobbin/optonic set-up is referred to repeatedly.

SUNDRIES

Split shot, that much publicized item of tackle should be of good design and material. Since legislation ruled that shot larger than, and including size 7, plus legers under and including 1oz must be of a non-toxic substance, there have been many types available to the angler. The less costly items are extremely hard, resulting in crushed line, and being immovable when placed. Far better to select the twin-cut pattern, which is soft enough to squeeze on to the line with two fingers; when the reverse sides are squeezed they become loosened. The thrifty angler will carefully remove these for future use.

Keepnets can be a bone of contention. A keepnet is necessary for the matchman, for he must weigh his fish at the end of a match. The pleasure angler, should he prefer not to use a keepnet, has added problems in the fact that in certain situations, a landed fish put back into the swim can be quite detrimental; in these cases, a keepnet is a must. The longest, widest net the angler can afford is advisable, made from micromesh, for some fish, barbel and carp in particular, have dorsal fins which are prone to becoming stuck in nets of a wide mesh.

Many years ago, I participated in a match on the Severn at Bewdley. Following the scalesmen along the bank, we came upon an angler who heaved his barbel-filled keepnet out of the water, struggling up the bank with over 20lb of fish. This was in the era of minnow-mesh nets, a period when the barbel of the Severn were still on the small side. The sorry sight of those young fish hung in the mesh like Christmas-tree decorations was too much for the angler. Without further ado he took out his knife, cutting the net to shreds in a successful bid to free the barbel. John Foster was his name, a Midlands match angler many could perhaps learn from. Shortly after this, micromesh keepnets became available, where today, to see even one barbel hung up is very rare indeed.

Conservation must be of prime concen for all anglers, so it may be advisable to leave a keepnet at home if at all possible. On many venues the angler will have no choice, where a keepnet ban is in force primarily for the good of the fish.

A good-sized landing-net is a must, the bigger the better. On venues where a shallow shelf drops off into deep water, it is most difficult to get a good heavy fish to come into the shallow water. The landing-net handle, therefore, should be strong and preferably of a three-piece extension, for this will give the angler a reaching range of over twelve feet.

Also in the area of conservation is hook removal. While the standard disgorger is adequate for small fish, a pair of good-class artery forceps is advisable to remove the hook from the mouth of a big fish, where any barb can be pushed down and backwards, resulting in clean removal.

Rod rests are too numerous to plough through. The leger man needs but one main consideration, that of selecting a head with a 'V' in the centre which will allow the line to run freely. The photo on this page shows a selection of leger heads, any of which will suffice.

There are many other items the well-equipped leger man will need: polaroid glasses, binoculars, target boards, bite indicators, catapults, an eye shield, sun cream, insect repellent, and more. To describe every single item an anger may require would fill another book; suffice to say that the basic necessities will be sufficient, all of which are dealt with within these pages where applicable.

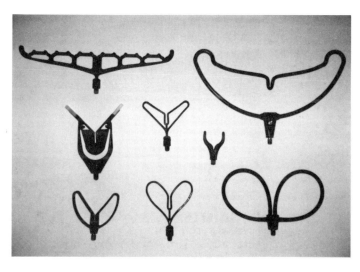

Selection of rod rests suitable for legering. Note all have 'V' recess for free-running line.

3   Baits

Before I commence with this chapter, I must stress the need for sensibility. I have yet to meet the angler who doesn't have a tale to tell of maggots escaping from the household fridge, and while this may have raised a few laughs, I doubt very much if the ladies of the respective houses carried the same views. I would therefore urge any serious angler to find a place in his shed or garage where he can put a bait fridge. I will guarantee he will enjoy a more placid life, saving pounds on keeping bait that would otherwise be thrown away.

Over the years, to the chagrin of my dear wife, and with distinct threat to the good health of my family, I have stored bait almost everywhere in my household. This led to heated arguments, also some interesting times with visitors – from a house suddenly full of acrid smoke from burning hempseed, to the time when a lady of the family went into my shed for a tin of paint. She knocked over a biscuit tin full of home-bred maggots…

There will always be certain baits associated with certain fish – bread for bream, cheese for chub, luncheon meat for barbel, and so on – but the truth is that any fish will eat just about anything. In my time, I have caught fish on some weird baits such as orange peel, baked beans, a bit of apple, and I must not forget the classic day when I took five chub on small pieces of bread pudding.

A caster/worm cocktail.

MAGGOTS

The plain old maggot continues to reign above all other baits. Every week of the season, thousands of gallons are poured into river, lake and canal countrywide, most of which are eaten, some of which crawl into mud and gravel, while the remainder simply rot. In the midst of this deluge, a maggot which stands out from others in the form of colour, taste, size or movement is bound to create some selective interest to fish.

Maggots from a reputable tackle dealer will be clean, almost smell-free and good enough to fish immediately. Should maggots be purchased in bulk, however, perhaps from a bait farm, they will need to be thoroughly cleaned before use, and this could apply also to bait which has been stored for any length of time.

A good riddle is necessary, obtainable from any tackle shop, though if any quantity is to be cleaned this could be on the small side. Should it be found that a larger one is necessary, the angler can make his own. A riddle of adequate size should be at least 2ft square, with a base of ⅛in wire mesh, preferably brass or some other non-rusting metal. The walls of the riddle need to be at least 6in high, and a catching box of similar proportions is also needed.

The bait is poured on to the riddle and left to pass through, repeated at least once more until all the rubbish has been removed. For the next part of the operation, the angler must move fast. Using about one pint at a time, the bait is poured on to the riddle, then quickly shaken from side to side above the box, where the remaining sawdust, etc. will be shaken through the riddle. Before the bait has time to move into the mesh, it is poured into a large bait container containing bran. The remainder of the bait is

given the same treatment, after which the rough nature of bran scours the bait, also carrying out a degreasing process; within a couple of hours the maggots will be as clean as you will need them. All that remains now is to give them a good sprinkle of ground maize meal and put them in a cool place, preferably a fridge.

Coloured maggots have been in vogue for many years, with the bronze colour the most popular. Not too many ago the most frequently used colouring was chrysodine, a powder dye that turns maggots a brilliant shade of translucent bronze. Fish reacted well to the colour, though I suspect their liking had something to do with the taste. Sadly, for both fish and angler, it became widely believed that chrysodine was conducive in promoting cancerous growth in humans, to the degree where coloured maggots were banned on many venues. Fact or not, I find it sad that there are old journals still available that recommend the use of chrysodine, and sadder still to know there are anglers around who follow this advice. With safer, equally

A selection of casters and maggots which a bream angler may need. The casters are kept in water to prevent them from 'turning' into floaters.

effective bronze colourings available, it is stupid to use this dye when everyone concerned, from manufacturers to tackle dealers, condemn the chemical as highly dangerous. Red, yellow, orange and green are all available from tackle shops in non-toxic dye form, and all are effective on their day.

While on the subject of maggots, there is one subject, an utter fallacy, which must be mentioned. All those years ago, when very few people owned a car, anglers travelled by bus or train. No sooner were they on the transport than out came the bait tins, to be to be placed under the air heaters to warm the maggots, making them wriggle to give more attraction. (Some went disgustingly further, putting a maggot into the mouth before mounting it on the hook.) I have never understood this. Whatever the temperature of the water may be, the bait should be colder than this wherever possible, thus when the maggot is thrown in it will liven up, wriggling away merrily. Once in colder water, however, a maggot which has been roasted, toasted or licked will probably die very quickly.

Gozzers

The art of selecting a bait for a particular species is most important, and this bait may need careful preparation. In this area of homework, perhaps more than anywhere else, anglers go to extreme lengths.

There are certain larvae of flies which, if raised and cosseted by the angler, can produce results when nothing else can. The gozzer, that ultra-perfect home-bred maggot so beloved by bream anglers, is a bait no serious angler should ignore. It can be bred to whatever size may be required, from a maggot almost twice as big as the shop-bought variety, to a tiny weevil associated with canal fishing. For the match angler, it is a must, for a bream will take a gozzer when it refuses any other bait.

The breeding of gozzers need not be the messy operation that it may at first appear. All that is required is a pig's heart or chicken breast from a butcher, a full-size biscuit tin, a pound of dry bran and a piece of muslin. The meat is left overnight for the 'blow' – the laying of the eggs by the fly. It is then put in the tin, covered by the bran, after which the muslin is tied over the top of the tin to prevent other flies laying more eggs. Five days later (or less, depending on how big you wish the bait to be) the bran is removed; the maggots will crawl from the feed which can then be discarded. Following two cleaning processes with bran dampened with milk, the gozzers will be big, pure white and extremely soft, a prime bait which no self-respecting bream can possibly ignore. There is something quite mysterious about the gozzer: it will raise bites from bream when the angler may think there is not a bream within a hundred yards.

Yet another special is the maggot bred on sour milk and bran, and while this may not be a serious bait for the leger angler to consider, the day will always arrive when the angler will wish 'if only I had some. . .'.

All that is needed is half a pint of ancient milk, a pound of bran and a shallow container. The milk is mixed with the bran to form a medium paste, put into the container to a depth of a couple of inches, and left to go rancid. Flies find this mess very quickly, and flies being what they are, lay their eggs. A crust forms rapidly on the surface, thus preventing evocative smells, and the container should be covered to prevent any further attacks by flies. Approximately one week later, the tin must be taken to somewhere a long way from home, preferably downwind, before being opened. The maggots should then be washed out with water, scoured in a fresh milk/bran mixture, and used within a couple of days.

Before concluding with fly larvae, this is a pertinent place to study the shape and movement. The blunt end of a maggot, complete with two dots which many think of as eyes, is widely believed to be the head; this is incorrect – it is the tail-end. This is where the maggot is hooked, but to shove a hook willy-nilly into the posterior of any maggot is asking for problems. If the maggot is gently squeezed from the pointed end, a protuberance becomes evident at the blunt end, and this is the vent of the maggot.

Try this exercise: place a maggot on a smooth surface and study its movement. You will see that at all times the vent protuberance is dragged along the surface, a position which never varies, for this is the natural way in which the larvae moves. Using a small hook, put it into this gristle with the point uppermost, after which the poor old maggot can wriggle away for all he is worth, dragging the hook behind him. In the fishing situation, the point of the hook will be well away from bottom debris, gravel and anything else which may prevent a fish being hooked. The maggot should just be nicked on, for if the hook is buried too deep there is a strong possibility it will curl over the hook, masking the point and preventing good penetration.

Feeder Maggots

Now we arrive at the feeders, the smaller maggots – smaller in size but certainly not in importance. The 'pinkie' is a very active little creature which can outlive its bigger cousin when submerged for long periods; by continuing to crawl around in a patch of groundbait it gives the all-important movement needed to generate interest. The pinkie is also useful as a hookbait when things are hard, perhaps on a freezing cold winter day when a big maggot dies within minutes of entering water – a pinkie will survive just that much longer. Care

must be taken when storing pinkies, for they can climb up any surface, especially if it is wet. A damp bait tin left open in a garage or shed will soon be devoid of pinkies, who won't take too long to buzz around in their hundreds.

The diminutive 'squat' is even smaller than a pinkie, and these larvae must be stored in damp sand to preserve them. They can be rather costly, but have a great effect on fish, especially bream. When added to groundbait or a swimfeeder, the squat can keep bream in a swim for a very long time, for bream grub about the bed, sorting out the tiny forms which do little to satisfy their appetite. The squat is also useful as a hookbait, but it is a desperate time indeed when a legerman has to stoop so low.

Casters

A caster is no more than the pupating chrysalis of the shop-bought big maggot. Casters are all important to the leger angler for, other than pike, I can think of no freshwater fish which cannot be caught on them. They are used in great quantities in bream and barbel fishing and, again, the preparation is vital. The caster needs to be in its early stage of transformation to the fly, for it is at this stage when it will sink. As the pupation process continues, the caster takes in air and floats, making it useless as a loose feed, though these floaters are excellent for hookbait as the weight of a hook is balanced by the buoyancy of the caster.

Casters purchased from a tackle dealer are normally fresh and large, but no dealer has the time or the inclination to prepare them to perfection; he sells in bulk and prepares his casters days in advance. Any angler who takes the trouble to 'turn' his own casters will go fishing knowing that his bait will be as fresh as is possible. To turn maggots into casters is a fairly simple process.

If the angler requires four pints of casters for a particular day, he needs to buy his maggots a week or so earlier, though this is variable at different times of the year, as maggots pupate faster in summer than in winter, Any reputable tackle dealer will sell a gallon of maggots which will produce fresh casters, and at a discounted bulk price. Ask the dealer for bait which will turn at the same time, and after giving them a good clean, put them into fresh, slightly damp sawdust. Settle them down in a cool spot, and after a day or two, light brown casters will be noticed among the maggots. These can be riddled off by putting the bait on to the riddle where they will crawl through; any which are left can be considered casters. These must be stored in an airtight bag or container, an essential factor to consider, for should the pupating bait be left in air, they will turn into floaters very quickly. When enough casters are gathered to make it worth your while, wash them in warm water with just a tiny amount of washing-up liquid to remove any last vestiges of smell or grease. To complete the process, give the whole lot a good swill in cold water, and dry them off by pouring them on to a few sheets of kitchen roll to absorb excess water.

After this they must be put in an airtight container such as a sealed bait tin, or even a polythene bag, but be careful with the latter as it is prone to being punctured.

WASP GRUB

Wasp grub, that bait which chub find so delicious, is a controversial subject. Banned by many angling organizations, it appears to be a bait predominant in the northern part of the country, where the media reports many matches won with wasp grub.

As the perfect example of just how effective grub can be, I must relate an experience from the past. In my match-fishing days I was a member of Camp A. C. of Worcester. In the late 1960s, the Camp won the Worcester & District A. A. Team Championships, winning all twelve sections using wasp grub as bait, a feat that has never since been repeated and probably never will be. Over one hundred nests were collected and used for this memorable occasion – a lot of work and a lot of pain.

When I was a lad there was only one way to obtain a wasp nest – or 'cake' as it is known – and that was to dig it out. The schoolboy method was to form a line of brave lads, all armed with a leafy bough of willow, who ran like demons to the hole, stopping to give it a bashing for a few seconds before running away, the odd one yelling in fear as he tore at his hair or shirt to squash a very angry wasp. Though stung many times, we had our precious 'whopper' grubs.

'Cymag' is a proprietary brand of wasp killer, but is cyanide based and somewhat dangerous in the wrong hands. A much safer method is to use balls of cotton wool soaked in tricoethylene (a liquid degreasing agent) which are safe, effective and harmless. This liquid gives off a powerful smell which can put a man into a well inebriated condition, and the effect it has on a wasp is much increased. The nest is found and checked for the number of entrances which are then marked with a piece of white paper. Late at night, when the wasps are in the nest, it's a simple operation to find each entrance, then to poke a piece of soaked cotton wool down each hole, covering it with earth. Come morning, with the wasps still and harmless – legless no doubt – the nest can be dug out. It's as simple as that.

Wasp-nest collecting is not for everyone. In these days of free enterprise, there are those who sell them at a fair price, men usually known to a tackle dealer, also pest control operatives who are constantly called in for nest removal by the public. Should you have a bait fridge with a freezer compartment, the nests can be preserved until required for winter use.

A wasp cake is set in layers, each layer composed of dozens of cells, each cell containing one grub. It is these grubs which chub go barmy for, large succulent larvae which have no parallel in the 'whopper-grub' season. Once enough grubs have been removed for hookbait, the remainder of the nest can be boiled, after which the excess water is removed before adding crumb to give it the consistency required for throwing in as groundbait. (I would advise that gloves be worn for this operation, for I swear a dead wasp can still sting.) It's best to prepare the mix on the evening previous to the day in question, for wasp cake is much like paper and needs a good soaking. The final product should be fairly heavy, each ball sinking quite a few feet before breaking up. The leger angler needs to make the mix very hard, allowing the balls to break up slowly on the bed of a river.

BREAD

Bread, without doubt, is the most under-rated, under-used bait I can think of. It is a bait which sorts out the bigger fish, for by virtue of its size a good-sized piece of flake or crust cuts out small fry; it is uncomplicated, effective for most fish yet many anglers continue to ignore it, which is quite surprising. There are few species which can refuse a well-presented piece of flake, and a thumbnail-size piece has accounted for many specimens.

A hook size is chosen for a particular species, perhaps a size 4 for carp, down to a 16 for roach. Breadflake must be mounted correctly for the best results, squeezed on to the shank and bend of the hook, with the point left hidden in the softer part of the bread; the edges can be left rough, allowing

fish to eat tiny portions as the edges break away. No preparation is required other than a few slices of a fresh sliced loaf. That part of a loaf not used can be frozen until required, when it is sealed in an air-tight bag and placed in a microwave oven for a few seconds, a sure way to make the slices moist once more.

Crust is by far the most effective bait for big chub. A whole loaf is required for this, one about two days old is ideal. The crust is picked out of the shell as needed. A piece the size of

A maggot surrounded by soft flake is a deadly cocktail for bream.

a 50 pence piece is not too big, into which a hook of balanced size, say 6–4, can be completely hidden.

WORMS

Yet another underrated bait is the plain old worm in its various forms, a bait completely free for collection. Lobs can be picked from a cut lawn by the dozen, preferably at night and with the aid of a torch. But be choosy where you visit. One dark night, when visiting a local golf-course I was surrounded by quite massive policemen who were informed that I was vandalizing the greens (the local Chief Superintendent was the Golf Club Captain).

Though worms may seem slow and brainless, they have a strong sense of self-preservation. Very rarely is all of a worm out of the hole, for the strong tail holds anchor, and should the flash of a torch be seen, or heavy footfall be sensed, you will see just how fast a worm can move – he'll go down his bolt hole like a rocket. The technique is to spot the worm, reach out a pointed finger, and before it withdraws trap the thing against the side of the hole. With the other hand, slowly withdraw the whole of the poor creature out of his hole, and pop it into a tin containing grass and damp earth.

That is summer worming. But how about in the depths of winter when a ground which is rock-hard could be covered in a foot of snow, hiding a glaze of ice, a time when lobworms are really good bait for chub, barbel and carp? Once again forward planning is needed, when enough worms are gathered in summer, and stored until winter. A wormery is required!

An old crock sink is just about unbeatable for this job, but as old crock sinks are not commonplace, a wooden box of 3ft or so square, 1ft deep, and of a decent thickness is completely adequate. It can be placed in the garden in a sunny corner, well out of the way of winds, washing lines, kids' scooters and inquisitive pets – for the aroma of a tomcat who has sprayed his territory is best avoided! Dig a hole up to 1ft deep, lay a piece of thick polythene or something similar on the bottom, place the box on this, fill it with plain old earth and you have a wormery. The excesses of a summer worm hunt will live quite happily in this environment, though it is perhaps necessary to cover the earth with leaf mould, or well-rotted garden compost to provide extra warmth.

Worms, like any other living creature, get hungry and must be fed. Potato peelings, tea bags or a handful of cornflakes a couple of times each week, even maybe a sprinkling of semolina pudding, will keep them fit until they are required. Should you become keen enough to turn the wormery over, and find anything dead, remove it at once. A dead worm gives off possibly the most awful smell imaginable.

Smaller redworms, those preferred by bream, will be found in well-rotted compost heaps or manure hills. There is another small worm of similar size known as a brandling, but these are not a good bait. True redworms can be identified by digging out a 'nest' – they will be found in clusters of twenty or so – and squeezing one or two. A redworm will exude red matter, while a brandling is striped and contains yellow matter. Redworms much prefer their habitat of wet manure when stored, which does not require any feed or upkeep other than keeping it free from frost. It must be stressed that storing worms for winter use is well worth the effort.

SEED BAITS

Hempseed, though rarely used as hookbait by a leger angler, is an attractor bait used in copious amounts. There is seed of different sizes on the market, and though I hear tales of Chilean hemp being the largest, I believe it is all to do with when the hemp was harvested, wherever it comes from; should Chileans harvest the plants late in the season, then I have no doubt it will be the biggest.

Roach, barbel, carp and tench are among the fish that respond well to a carpet of hempseed, but before it can be used it needs to be cooked. Many tackle shops now sell freshly cooked hempseed over the counter, though by far the most economical method is to buy it dry in bulk from a seed merchant, cooking amounts as required.

An easy way of cooking hemp is to fill a third of an old pressure cooker with seed, fill it to within an inch of the top with cold water and let it soak for a day. In this manner the seed will swell to almost double its dry size, and when brought to the boil and left overnight, the angler will have half as much again in bulk as when he started. What is not required immediately can be frozen in polythene bags and kept for months, if not years; a couple of minutes in a microwave will soon put the seed into usable form.

If a fishing trip is planned the day after boiling hemp, the water from the pot will be of great value as a groundbait mixer. After removing the boiled hemp with a fine-mesh scoop it will be seen that thousands of tiny white particles are left in the water; these are the kernels of the seed which fish find delicious. Globules of oil can be seen on the surface, oil which is one of the greatest attractors of fish I know, especially for barbel. The water should be left to cool before mixing, adding brown or white cereal (and sometimes both) until the groundbait is of a nice fluffy mix, though with a consistency which hardens when squeezed tighter. This is mandatory when legering in any depth, or when using an open-end feeder, for it is necessary to keep the groundbait solid until it reaches the bottom.

Another way of preparing hempseed is to cook it, and then liquidize a pint or two in a food processor. This will result in a sticky grey mess, but when mixed with just a small portion of white cereal is tremendously effective, either packed in a feeder or fed in lump form. This, I find, is most effective in the search for big roach and chub, when the use of normal cereal groundbait can be self-destructive.

Tares are a bird food connected with hempseed and, though normally associated with trotting a float for summer roach, can be deadly when legered correctly. Tares must also be boiled before use and, yet again, it is wise to soak them in cold water to soften them before boiling. There is no definite time attached to this, it's a matter of simmering until a few seeds can be flattened when squeezed between finger and thumb. When they reach this stage, remove them from the boil and swill them in cold water; they are then ready for use. Many anglers stir in a teaspoonful of bicarbonate of soda before boiling to help soften the seed, but personally I believe this is unnecessary and could leave a taint. Tares can be frozen, but lose much of their effectiveness; nor can they be stored because they will begin to ferment and smell 'vinegary'.

Sweetcorn is another bait which just about any fish will eat; it is a wonderfully simple bait which is purchased in tins from a grocer. Open the tin and use it – it's as simple as that. Some anglers take the trouble to treat sweetcorn by soaking it in aromatic dyes, such as strawberry flavourings, banana, lemon, and a host of other additives, and they probably catch more fish in doing so. I am, however, a great believer that fish eat sweetcorn because of its natural taste. It is a bait which can take time to be effective, where the angler must have confidence and patience. At length, and with everything else in his favour, he will – if he is lucky – catch fish.

A net of small roach taken on legered tares.

BOILIES

Boilies are a specialized bait associated with the carp angler, though tench also show a great liking for small boilies. While I would not dream of delving into the secret recipes of the carp specialist, it may be pertinent at this stage to give some idea of just how much trouble these dedicated anglers will take in looking for a new bait which catches. Their difficulties lie in the fact that carp, above all of our fish, become very wary of a bait which has taken its toll.

The boilie is much like groundbait: it is a carrier. The enticement lies in the dozens of additives, plus any amount of various oils. To sum up, there are many, many flavours which are tried, used for a while, to be discarded as they become less effective. There are a number of reputable firms marketing boilies, many of them headed by proven carp anglers. I have

no doubt that all are excellent, marketing a range of flavours too numerous to be listed in this book, but yet again I have the sneaking suspicion that the carp angler can become utterly confused in his selection as there are so many.

There are other baits for the leger angler to consider, dealt with as the individual species are examined; most will be for the specialist or specimen hunter. Cheese has long been associated with chub, barbel and carp, while luncheon meat, too, is considered a specialist bait for the same species. These baits are covered in later chapters.

A thinking angler can beat out his brains trying new things, smelling out the house, even being reported by neighbours. This is all part of being a fisherman. The constant search for that secret, never-before-used bait is paramount, though it will remain effective or secret for such a short period. I have been involved in this search for as long as I can recall, discovering at times a bait which catches a few bonus fish, but most times I failed miserably. I wouldn't have missed it for the world.

Baits are not only for catching fish. Certain magazines, more so those from abroad, carry adverts of a brand new, scientific, truly magical discovery, a bait so devastating it is guaranteed to have fish rushing from miles away to get at it, a bait so irresistible that you will never need anything else. The angler new to the sport is a sucker for this promise, but take my advice, there is no such bait around. Don't believe a word of it – don't get caught!

4   Swimfeeders

The swimfeeder must be the most devastating item of tackle to affect modern angling. From the days of straight legering with quiver, spring or swingtip, etc., 99 per cent of anglers now plump for the feeder. The reasons for this are numerous, but the angler need look no further than the fact that the feeder method in its basic form is simple, usually instant, and very, very effective.

My good friend Keith Arthur of London claims to be the joint inventor of the block-end swimfeeder. The open-end had been around for some time before Keith and a colleague experimented with a piece of thick plastic sheet drilled with holes. The following passage is an edited version of the progress of events as told to me by Keith.

An angler named Bill Branch had something secret, for his catches of dace were simply phenomenal; he also caught more than his fair share of barbel. The allegation was that 'Twiggy' had feeders that needed no groundbait, no doubt the reason for his success with dace.

I started to work on this, along with two colleagues, Billy Allen and Billy Harris, but could find nothing better than gluing one end of a standard feeder shut, and using crumb in the other end to hold the maggots in. We caught significantly more dace, even the odd barbel, but reached nowhere near the amount caught by Mr Branch.

Eventually, it all came to light. Twiggy worked as a plastic moulder, and had crafted a mould to produce heavy perspex tubes, slotted, with a one-piece bottom. A top cap was made to fit snugly inside, and this is where the elastic bands came into play. Once the maggots were pushed inside the tube, the elastic band went through the lid, then through the bottom of the feeder, where it was held in place by half a matchstick.

We had no access to plastic moulds, but a model shop sold sheet perspex for model aircraft windows, and a leather punch to make the holes. For lids we ordered 1,000 empty shot boxes. Our local tackle dealer, Mr Whaley, thought we had gone mad, but at 3d each, £12 10s was not to be sneezed at! Our punctured perspex was rolled until it fitted snugly into the boxes, after which they were stapled together. The unstapled lids were the tops of the shot boxes which could be opened and closed easily.

Sheet lead was no problem as another of our pals worked for the local electricity board, and in those days their copper cable was wrapped in sheet lead. Any surplus cable was stripped, and the lead used in our feeder workshop.

These 'blockends' as they became known, weighed about 2½oz empty, and as there were no purpose-made rods available, heavy glass spinning rods were commonplace; bite indicators were definitely surplus to our requirements, for the rod would often be almost wrenched from our hands. It was soon obvious that we were on to a winner. Trials proved that anything less than 5lb line was broken by dace on the bite. We found that a size 12 hook was certainly not too big for this method, where a single maggot was by far the best bait.

Our first match with the blockend was in the L.A.A. Knockout Shield, where we competed against a team which had a long reputation of success on the Thames. We held high hopes of doing well – but just how well was almost too good to be believed. Results of the Shield event were decided by a fish count, only going to the scales if there was no decisive outcome, though it was soon evident that scales would not be necessary! The final score was our 119 fish – 108 dace, 8 roach, 3 barbel – to their 3. A rout!

That was enough for the L.A.A. An emergency meeting was called, and the late Reg Cooke, ultimately destined to become Chairman, proposed a motion that these 'infernal machines' be banned.

These were the first production models of the original blockend, and the basic design has changed very little over the ensuing years. Streamlining has helped, and of course fish have grown wiser, where the use of sensitive quiver tips and other bite indicators are now essential.

Such was the impact of the feeder as recalled by Keith Arthur, recognized as one of today's leading feedermen. Today, if you went to the Thames with 5lb line, tied direct to a size 12 hook baited with a single maggot and waited for a dace to pull the rod off the rest, you would still be there at the turn of the century. But if you can find a river that holds dace which have never seen a blockend, give it a try. One never knows, it may result in further days of wine and roses.

For years, the feeder remained a tactic used only by southern anglers. We of the Midlands, plus anglers further north, all justly proud of our float and quiver-tipping skills, looked upon it as quaint at best, ridiculously cumbersome at worst, treating our southern counterparts as piscatorially backward. How wrong we were.

In the September of 1956, the then Severn River Board, in conjunction with the *Angling Times*, introduced barbel to the Severn. This original stocking comprised of fish removed from the River Kennet in Berkshire, long the home of specimen barbel (trout, too, a good reason for removing barbel). Sixty-four fish were released at Bridgnorth, Hampton Loade and Arley, with other releases along the length of the river, totalling 509. The biggest

Fishing the feeder on the Severn. Fred Bailey waits with arms folded for a fish to hook itself.

of these barbel weighed 9lb, and though the odd fish was reported in forthcoming seasons, it took over ten years for them really to establish themselves, and into the early 1970s before they began to be caught in any quantity. Predictably, the day arrived when someone somewhere, perhaps a holiday-maker from 'darn sarf' who, knowing no other method, fished the feeder. That was *it*! Virtually overnight, 100lb bags of fish were winning matches, with pleasure anglers catching twice that amount. The barbel were small, with the big bags comprising fish around the 1–2lb mark, a 4lb fish being the rarity.

The rest is history. In no time at all, anglers, realizing the feeder was unbeatable for catching barbel, looked upon it as the first method to try, and for some, the only one. At birthdays or Christmas, kids were treated to a leger rod, a cheap ready-filled reel, a gift pack of a dozen big blockends and a packet of eyed hooks. With this tackle – and I do not exaggerate – off they popped to the Severn and hauled out bag after bag of barbel to more than 50lb. What nipper would want to do anything else?

The day of the Instant Angler had befallen the Midland float artists. Specialist matchmen were born, men who never moved off the Severn, becoming known nationally as ton-up anglers – those who had won with more than 100lb.

The face of match and pleasure angling in the Midlands changed dramatically over the next few years. Where it was once difficult to obtain a ticket for any match, they were now readily available at the draw. To quote an instance, the Kidderminster & District A.A. stretch at Bewdley was once a venue where the winner would come from just about anywhere, depending on who drew what peg and how many mistakes – if any – he made. Each match was akin to a 1st Division National where every other peg was being fished by a household name, anglers from Lancashire to London. Ashurst, Marks, Smith, Giles, Moult, Winter and Mumford – all men who were top of their sport – came to the Severn to demonstrate their skills. Stick float, waggler, straight legering, roach, dace, chub, bleak, were factors once in the reckoning at all matches. Then came the feeder.

There are now less than fifteen winning pegs at Bewdley, where on a normal summer or autumn river, an angler who doesn't have 10lb in his net after an hour can go to watch someone who has. The remainder of the river follows a similar pattern, each venue showing the favourite haunts of the barbel. These pegs are well known to the match or pleasure angler, the latter very aware that if a match is not taking place, he will need to be awake early to find a vacant peg.

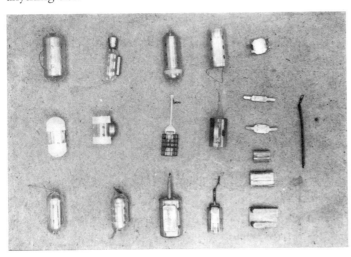

A small selection of swimfeeders. The range of strip leads are attached to vary the amounts of weights as required.

Max Winters, an old Cofton and Birming-ham A.A. colleague, tried the method once, winning by a large margin. He summed up his feelings by stating – and I quote – he could 'teach a schizophrenic chimpanzee how to fish the feeder in half an hour'. Max spoke the thoughts of many top Severn match anglers, who, as a result of the outcome depending on the draw rather than on the skills of the angler, left the river, never to return.

The story didn't end on the Severn. At the time, the Hampton Ferry waters on the War-wickshire Avon at Evesham were the mecca for Midland match anglers. Hampton Ferry is a slow, dreamy part of the river where roach were once predominant, where huge chub swam lazily two feet down in 12ft of water, and where in times of spate a match would be won with 2lb of bleak. In contrast to the con-trary moods of the Severn, the approach needed to catch fish at Evesham demanded the ultimate in finesse and bait presentation; as such, anyone who wanted to make a name for himself had to perform well over a long period. Some of today's international anglers spent their apprenticeship at Evesham, and other top anglers, too.

In the ranks of Cofton A.C. was one Bill Stroud. Fresh from a run of wins on the Sev-ern, Bill sat down to consider the possibility of fishing the feeder on the Avon. Virtually immediately, he put together a string of wins,

including 20lb nets of chub from pegs where chub were not known to live. Big bream came to the net, plus many roach of over 1lb which, although not a rarity, were considered to be in the domain of the float angler. Thus the Avon also fell to the feeder. The method spread to the Trent and to the Wye, both rivers where the float once reigned supreme.

I paint this picture purposely to demon-strate the impact of the swimfeeder in the 1970s. It was decried as unskilled, a spoiler, and would be detrimental to fish and fishery. Happily, attitudes changed. The deeper-thinking anglers, realizing the advent of an angling era, picked up the basics, improving them to degrees of finesse so far unimagined.

Tackle firms, happy that a new method had arrived which demanded new items of tackle, introduced mini-feeders, capable of taking and distributing slowly no more than a dozen maggots. The Drennan firm marketed their famous range of Feeder-links, a perfect answer to the delicate demands of winter roach, when to loose feed one handful of maggots or cast-ers too much was asking for disaster. Block-ends became available in three sizes – small, big and huge – though many anglers, feeling these were still not big enough, manufactured their own from a variety of food tins.

Far from being confined to the Thames, the open-end method was used on other venues, where the angler could now put his hookbait and groundbait to one spot, concerned no more that a thrown ball of groundbait may break into a dozen pieces in the air, splitting the shoals as it fell in a line between bank and leger. Thus almost every application of leg-ering could be covered in one way or the other by a swimfeeder. Today, in the hands of the better anglers – match, pleasure or speci-men hunter – the swimfeeder method in all its forms now covers a multitude of approaches, many of which demand the very best in skills and angling ability.

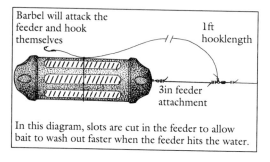

In this diagram:

Barbel will attack the feeder and hook themselves

1ft hooklength

3in feeder attachment

In this diagram, slots are cut in the feeder to allow bait to wash out faster when the feeder hits the water.

Fig. 4 Matchmans' baitless barbel rig.

BLOCKEND FEEDER

The blockend is no more than a plastic tube full of holes, blocked at both ends, one of which should have a removable cap for filling purposes. It is used when groundbait is not desirable, and contains samples of hookbait and other attractors such as hempseed. There are many firms marketing feeders of all descriptions, but all that is required of a blockend is to put the bait where the angler wishes, having enough lead to make it stay put, and to allow the enclosed bait to escape, preferably after it has reached the bottom. To accomplish this, the holes should be large enough to let maggots wash through, but not too big where they fall out in mid-flight. I often find the manufacturers make the holes purposely on the small size, and it's up to the angler to make them larger if he wishes; if they are too large in the first place, there is nothing much anyone can do.

For fast-water fishing, with big fish such as chub or barbel in mind, the unwary angler will use the biggest of the blockends, for these species can normally eat as much bait as can be put into the river. But he should be careful. If there is any residue, it is quickly washed away, and if the angler continues to introduce excessive bait into his swim, the fish will quickly follow it. Smaller sizes of blockend are used where the pace of water is more gentle, for it is in such places that fish demand a slightly more subtle approach.

The amount of lead used with any feeder is of utmost importance, and it is in this area

Mid-Severn barbel country at Arley.

that most problems occur. No manufacturer can supply a feeder for every occasion, for every swim on any river in the country can differ from day to day, sometimes from hour to hour. Unless he has the tackle and knowledge to overcome this, an unprepared angler will tear out his hair in exasperation. What is needed here are trim leads, pieces of lead which can be attached to the feeder in seconds. In this way, a perfect weight can be attained which can be changed at will as conditions demand.

An item of tackle known as the snap-link swivel is used for speed, where it is attached to a lead or a feeder, clipping into place. For some, it is well worth the few extra pence it costs, although it is disliked by others for the increased possibility of tangles; personally, I dislike anything which is unnecessary hardware, especially if it requires an excessive amount of knots. Therefore, through-out the remainder of this book, I leave the use of the snap-link to the personal tastes of the angler.

To attach the feeder, 6in or so of reel line is tied to it using a tucked half blood knot, to which a swivel is secured, the reel line being threaded through the eye. Another development is to use a length of power gum – a form of elasticized line – covered with silicone tubing. These forms of feeder link can either be allowed to run up and down the reel line, stopped with a leger stop, or multi-turn knot with a small shot pinched directly on top, or tied into a large bow to give better bite registration. There are more variations of link attachment which some anglers swear by, some quite unnecessarily complicated.

The cone-shaped feeder is designed for use on moving water, where its shape gives less resistance. The reel line passes through the centre of the feeder, stopped by a split shot on both sides. If these shot are placed close to the feeder, with no more than three inches of free line, it becomes a 'bolt' rig as used by carp anglers. The theory of a bolt rig is to allow a

fish to take the bait, and when it feels the resistance of the terminal tackle – in this case a feeder – it bolts; the weight then sets the hook.

Also in this category is the tubed Drennan Feeder-Link, a mini-version of the blockend. Where a small blockend will carry only a few maggots or casters, these are still far too many for the hard days of winter, when fish must be tempted with very few free samples. The Drennan design of tube feeder-link is superb

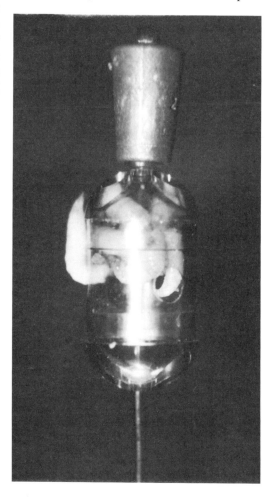

A cut-down Drennan Feeder-Link holding six maggots.

for this form of fishing, holding as few loose feed samples as is desired. It can be made smaller still, simply by cutting through the body with a sharp knife, reducing the length as necessary. The feeder-link is balanced by adding or taking off shot on the tail of line hanging from the bottom of the feeder. The slightly bigger versions have interchangeable weights to cope with varying depths and flow. They can be changed by squeezing the two feet together and withdrawing the legs, after which the chosen weight is clipped in place. This type of feeder falls to the bottom in the upright position, thus keeping the attachments free from any chance of tangling.

OPEN-END FEEDER

The open-end feeder, again nothing more than a tube with holes in it, is used to deliver groundbait to a required spot in the swim. The ideal is to mix groundbait as dry as possible, though with enough consistency for it to hold together. After a few seconds in the water, the groundbait takes in water and expands, freeing itself from the feeder. Though modern groundbaits are sometimes garnished with aromatic additives, the main purpose is as the carrier for hookbait samples. Should casters be the choice of feed, all that is required is for a handful to be added to the groundbait, mixing well before the feeder is pushed into the groundbait bowl and filled. Maggots are different inasmuch they wriggle, and must be put into the centre of the feeder between two packed ends. (Chapter 8 deals with this in more detail.)

CAGE FEEDER

Before the cage feeder was available on the market, and in spite of strange looks, I bought packs of hair curlers – a perfect cage of thin plastic, into which groundbait could be packed tightly. The commercial wire cage feeder is more or less the same shape, with lead added.

The cage feeder empties much quicker than an open-end version, though care must be taken in casting. Any jerking motion on the cast results in the groundbait falling out in mid-air, therefore a slow continuous swing is needed, feathering the feeder to the water. To strike against an empty cage feeder is to think it has fallen off, for by its very design it has almost no resistance. When striking at short distance, therefore, care needs to be taken: it should be treated as a straight link-ledger without any feeder attachment. Another quirk of the cage feeder is that the hook only has to touch it to become snagged, and because of this factor many anglers are loath to use it. But it does have its uses, limited though they may be.

LIFTING FEEDER

No more than a variation, this item is deliberately designed to lift in the water on retrieve. Apart from this, it does nothing different from anything else, but the lifting abilities are very useful, more so when fishing over lilies or weed beds on shallow stillwaters.

There are many, many more varieties and designs of feeders available, but all are based on the foregoing. There are no secrets. All that is required is a bit of common sense when balancing the feeder in moving water, and when choosing the feeder to do the job in question. I am in no doubt that as anglers attempt to invent new rigs, with weird combinations of loops, swivels and beads, they become their own enemies. The swimfeeder is a very simple method, complicated only by its users.

5 The Meat Method

The method of fishing with meat as bait is not new; it has been around for over a hundred years. Raw beef was used to catch eels as long ago as the late 1800s, with big lumps hung on massive hooks tied to horsehair string, and left tethered to the bank overnight.

The bait, albeit in another form, came back to prominence in the years from about 1965 onwards, a chuck-and-chance-it method used when all else failed. My interest was born in that as a match angler, I could never come to terms with the fact that on the prolific Severn, winter matches, or matches held in times of spate, were won with less than 5lb. After months of head-aching trial and error, I developed a method of fishing for big weights in times of high water, which resulted in many wins and a lot of big fish. I became a specimen-hunting matchman.

At the time, barbel were not prominent in the Severn; everyone knew they were there, but very few were caught. Besides which, we anglers of the West Midlands, unused to barbel, thought of them purely as a summer fish which spent their days in the clear, weed-filled chalk streams of southern England, unheard of after the cool of autumn. My target, therefore, was chub: they were in the river in massive shoals, along all stretches, with insatiable appetites.

In order to catch them, I devised a method that will help any angler to overcome the many problems that are encountered when using a specific bait to catch a specific fish. I believed that to hook big chub, specifically, bait should be on the large size. Not that chub would take only a large bait – but it did rule out the smaller 'nuisance' fish. For this kind of bait, the hook size needed to be much larger than the matchman's maggot or caster patterns. Line, too, had to be stepped up from the normal 1.7lb b/s reel line and 1.1lb hooklength. Only trial and error would determine these factors, so all was fairly simple so far. But what about the rod? What length should I look for – how stiff, how heavy, etc.?

One day whilst out practising – I forget where – a man who introduced himself as Pat stopped for a natter, and within minutes we were on the subject of rods. Amongst other things, we talked of missed bites and striking; before he left, promising me a meat rod to end all meat rods.

Eventually it arrived, nine feet long, extremely heavy, with a top joint made of solid glass; I believe it cost me a tenner and a pint. I'll be forever grateful to Pat, for that chance meeting was conducive to the success which followed.

I caught fish with the rod, though after a few trips it became obvious that things were still not right, but at least I had a pattern. I tramped once more around many tackle shops, searching for a similar blank, though one which was hollow, slightly longer and certainly much lighter. Eventually I found it, a 9½ft hollow glass North Western blank, which complete with finished butt cost around £5.00. I cut 3in from the top, and 4in off the butt, including the cork. After applying rings with tape, and fishing for less than an hour, I knew that this was *it*! It was light, stiff, bent well and I caught more fish per bite ratio than ever before. I whipped on some rings in the form of the Fuji three-legged match type. The Meatmaster (the rod!) was born and I looked no further. But still I missed too many bites.

Initially, I used a massive size 6 of a popular canal hook, the old Mustad 39082. The pattern details stated 'Sproat hook. 3 ex. fine wire, extra short shank wide gape spade end' – one would think not the ideal for big fish; but few fish came off those hooks once on. I believe the design did the unique job of actually closing the gape when the fish pulled. However, as is usual when life is good, the rainbow disappeared when Mustad decided to discontinue this hook in sizes larger than 14. Eventually another hook was discovered in the form of the Mustard 496, a 'reversed' hook, which in layman's terms means nothing more than bent sideways. It has a wide gape, is short shanked, with a point that remains sharp.

The brand of meat had also to be considered. When a river is in spate it is murky, and fish feed by smell alone. To use a cheap smell-less make resulted in less bites. After experimenting with various brands, a particular make came to the fore, that of chopped ham with pork. This mixture has a higher than usual salt content and, with the added fats of pork, produced what I believed to be the best available [I still do!]. I would hazard a guess that fish can't really distinguish one luncheon meat from another, and despite the number of tins thrown into rivers, they can't read the details on the label either. Later, perhaps with good reasoning, many anglers reckoned I used some secret bait additive. But that was just wild guessing – honest!

During those periods when the river was so cold that the meat came back intact, I experimented with meat paste. Adding cornflower, I kneaded the meat in a bowl with a potato masher until it reached a putty-like consistency. After leaving it in a fridge all night it was perfect as hookbait for the following day. The experimenting was well worth while, for bites materialized with paste, when to use meat from the tin resulted in many a dry net. (Such was the success of this paste that in later years, Clive Smith, captain of Cofton Hackett, appointed me paste maker for the team. On one particular winter league event, held on the Severn at Atcham, anyone who sat with the paste throughout caught fish. Two didn't – they had dry nets.)

Just a small selection of meats that will catch fish. All that is needed is a tin opener.

THE MEAT METHOD

For the first practice trips I chose periods when the river was really unfishable as regards float techniques – times of rain, snow and general rough weather, but for my purposes quite perfect. Within fifteen minutes' drive from my home I could take my pick of good venues along the Severn or Teme, but invariably I fished the weir at Holt Fleet. I knew it to be stuffed with fish but, perhaps more to the point, it is just six minutes from home with a pub within easy walking distance. Both of these factors were necessary for my purposes, as this early self-training period was spent mostly at night.

The reason for this was simple. All anglers know that fish feed better during the hours of darkness. It was of little use attempting to develop the method during the daytime, struggling to raise a bite, when a session during the night could produce bites one after the other for hours on end. Naturally, the resulting fish were not all specimens by any means, although I had my share of big chub and, in later years of course, big barbel. This early period of night fishing proved to be invaluable, for in the following years I caught more fish by sensing the bite than in any other way. (Bream, too, developed a taste for meat, but were to all intents and purposes a nuisance as the bite could only be hit when the fish had whittled down the size of the bait.)

It became obvious that fish could be caught in quantity using the method, even when the river carried several feet of flood water, but the main problem became glaringly apparent in that from every ten bites, I managed to hit an average of about one.

One of the major causes was a leger that rolled on the bottom. At first I considered this a bonus for I was able to cover more ground. After a while, however, I realized a static bait was required, for it was my view that in conditions of spate, not many fish would be darting all over the place actually competing for food. Therefore, the leger needed to be looked at.

Though Dick Walker was an angling giant, his Arlesey bomb, designed for perch fishing at long distance in Arlesey Lake, proved to be inadequate for river fishing. On a river carrying up to six feet of swiftly moving flood water an Arlesey bomb rolled, needing a size of ridiculous proportions to hold bottom. The answer to this problem was simple. When under sideways pressure, things which are round roll – flat objects don't! Out came the hammer and a few belts soon had a couple of bombs looking like something I thought more appropriate. A 1oz flattened lead did the job which took a standard 2oz bomb, while a ½oz size did the job of a 1oz and so on. With the old brain now in gear I hammered out a set of Arlesey bombs which transformed wholly my ideas on legering.

Try this exercise. Place a 2oz bomb on a flat surface. Blow hard at it, and you will find it will roll. Put a ¼oz coffin lead next to it and repeat the exercise – this I think is a fair representation of water action on the leger.

The *amount* of lead was also critical. From the outset, I'd been thinking of just how much lead was required to hold bottom, which was in fact altogether wrong. What actually happens is that the bottom stops the lead, therefore the bottom *holds* the lead, not the reverse. Admittedly, a heavy lead will of course sit *on* the bottom, but even a tiny lead can be held *by* the bottom should it settle at a twig, a stone or any other minor snag. This was a major step.

Line was the next consideration. Using 2.6 breaking strain line, I could hold bottom using a ½oz lead, even with a couple of feet of flood on the river. However, this proved to be on the light side, for I was occasionally broken, especially when a fish took the rod almost off the rest. Still using my favourite Bayer Perlon, I upped it to 3.2lb b/s, which almost solved the problem, although at times the lead had greater difficulty in holding bottom with the extra diameter of the line. If this problem arose I added a swan shot to the link, changing to the next size lead upwards if necessary. At length I settled for 4.4lb line with which I reckoned I could land the *Queen Mary*.

If an angler were to sit at any peg along the river Severn, from Wales to the Bristol Channel, and cast out a leger rig with a lump of meat on his hook, sooner or later – it may be weeks – the rod will go round. This will result in either a hooked fish, a broken line, a missed 'bite' or a disappearing rod. It is imperative with this method to attend to the rod at all times, for it will do neither fish or angler any good at all if the fish pulls the rod from the rest and tows it around the river for a day or two. This has happened many times on the Severn, and rods are lost forever; it still happens to this day. A quick lesson here may be prudent. Never leave a cast rod unattended – you may not see it again.

But is such a heaving round of the rod a bite? I don't think so. Not for one moment do I consider that *any* fish – roach, chub, bream or barbel – need to pull the rod tip round two feet to eat a bait. What I think happens is this. The fish approaches the bait with the usual self-preserving caution, smelling, tasting the aroma from a distance. If all is well, it may mouth the bait; such as a barbel will use its barbules to taste the offering. Then, should the bait be loose feed, it will take it in and scoff it! Wonderful, thinks Mr Chub (or Mr Barbel), if indeed a fish can think at all – which I doubt – and off he glides to the next bit. The same procedure will follow, until the time will come when the bait may have a hook in it. He smells, tastes, takes in the bait and feels the hook. His minute brain screams RUN! In a flash he is off, but the hook, or maybe the bait if it is big enough, sticks in his

mouth, and he pulls the rod round where he either hooks himself or flees in terror. This is the 'unmissable' bite that gives the angler nightmares, a walloping round of the rod which, if resulting in a hooked fish, is a matter of pure luck. It is obvious that the actual bite – the moment when the fish takes the bait confidently into its mouth – happens long before this. So in the initial evaluation of this delicate bite, the problem was to determine where the peak of the biting process occurred – the very moment when the fish took the bait in its mouth.

Eventually, after much striking at what I thought may have been bites but probably weren't, my mind wandered to the days of black mollies, kissing gouramies and the like – to the happy hours I spent watching my tropical fish take in tiny morsels, only to spit them out in an instant should they be inedible. No doubt this happened with meat, maggots and probably every other bait one could think of: in a fish's mouth and out in less than a blink. Logic said I received many bites on my bits of meat that I knew nothing about. The whole process now depended upon my picking them out.

The tip of the joint was much too thick to show any form of normal bite, and it was here perhaps that my thinking differed from the norm. Quiver tips were almost always built into the blank, so continuing the rod action. This was all very nice for bream or roach, but the method which I was trying to perfect didn't require such finesse. I reckoned a screw-in tip would be more sensible, inasmuch as once the bite was detected by a movement of the tip, then it was out of the game, it didn't do anything. And nor did I want it to. When a bite resulted in a hooked fish, all initial pressure was put on the top ring of the rod, the line going in a straight line right down to the hook. I chose a 8in tapered tip, glued into the threaded adaptor which is

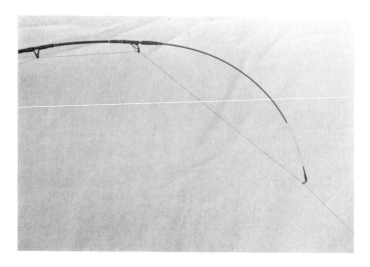

A screw-in quiver tip under pressure. All the weight is taken from the top ring of the rod.

universal to threaded tip rings. With this refinement the catch rate improved – but not enough.

Angles were the next consideration. How long the hooklength, how much line did the lead-link need? After a lot of sliding of shot up and down the reel line I arrived at the conclusion that a 2:1 ratio was perfect, for example a 6in lead-link to a 12in hooklength. With these measurements I felt I could make the meat dance around a little without moving the lead, so inducing a bite or two. When the bite occurs, the fish moves the finely balanced leger, the bait goes easier into its mouth, the pressure goes from the tip which flies back, giving the now well-known drop-back bite – only it's an extremely fast process and it all happens in a flash.

Almost overnight I upped the catch rate by fifty per cent. Once I had this picture firmly established in my mind – the movement of the tackle from bite to tip movement – the results went up splendidly. One further problem arose when breaks in the line became a regular occurrence. I made the usual examination

of the rings, changing the line to a stronger breaking strain, etc. without success. I still got broke.

The problem had manifested itself during a match held on Winnals, a deeper part of the Severn below Stourport. At the end of the match – I didn't bother to weigh in – I hurried down the meadows to see how Ken Giles had fared. Not very well would be a fair definition; Ken's words, however, were much more descriptive for he caught one gudgeon, and not a very big one at that. To all intents, the match was a disaster, being won with less than double figures, but forever the optimist I thought I'd have a crack on the meat at my friend's peg. I fished for about half an hour. I landed a pair of chub for 2lb, missed four bites and was broken twice. I felt no sense of triumph, but the result confirmed my feelings that fish, if there were any around, would feed if given the right grub at the right time using the right method.

But what of those missed bites? How about the breaks? The line was okay, so where was the fault? At the time I used the old red Abu 505 reel, modified by the removal of the grotesque star wheel by which the angler adjusted the drag setting, and by the removal, too, of the internal drag setting, preferring to allow the reel to turn backwards when a fish was running. All this changing of design had been made specifically with meat fishing in mind, and I believe the reel was right, but what I had overlooked was the strain put on the line at the point where the pick-up pin made contact with it. On a strike, which with this method is necessarily hard, the only place where a weak spot can feasibly be is at this pin,

To prevent reel line from breaking on the pick-up pin, the line is cushioned against the finger on the strike.

closed- or open-faced reels, I let the line rest on my little finger. Upon a firm strike the line presses against the finger taking the shock. I have never since been broken at the reel, or indeed on the strike.

During these nocturnal practices at Holt Fleet I became aware of dangers peculiar to the night fisher. I was snarled at by a mangy dog fox, assaulted many times by cows, dive-bombed by bats and hit by a bottle thrown into the river by an idiot. None of these, however, distracted me from the dire need to catch fish.

and it was here that the line was breaking. The reason was that the line, touching this pin immediately it left the reel, had no room to stretch with its natural elasticity. From that day, whenever I fish with meat, using either

With the rig and method now as near perfect as they ever would be, I added one more refinement by standing at all times. This may seem unnecessary, but it is my firm conclusion that an angler, standing comfortably with the rod pointed at the bait, held up at an angle of somewhere near forty-five degrees, will hook more fish than in any other stance. Upon a bite, all that is required is a bend of the knees, a lightning-fast bending of the elbow, which means a walloping over the shoulder with the rod. Any other method or stance is detrimental to the overall picture and should not be tolerated. (Of course, it's a game for a fit young man, and not for a second do I think I could do it now. But in those heady times I could

Standing whilst meat fishing keeps the maximum of line out of the water.

THE MEAT METHOD

After a few biteless hours the author smiles for the camera.

stand for five hours in snow, rain or thunder, freezing or steaming hot days, detecting at times just one bite for a good pay packet or a win for a team.)

A warning! The method is virtually unbeatable on days when the river is out of order, when float or feeder tactics cannot be applied. But when the river is of good colour and level, fish see every item of tackle, from lead to line, and the meat will not get a look in. Wait for the rains, or perhaps fish at night and you may feel as I did all those years ago – you will feel you can walk on water.

Such is the harrowing tale of how the meat method came to prominence. In its basic form, and on a river which holds chub or barbel, the method can win most winter matches. For the pleasure angler, or specimen hunter, meat accounts for the majority of reported specimen barbel, succeeding on a grand scale when other methods fail miserably.

Today, the barbel of the Severn grow to massive proportions, can be quite cunning and require stronger tackle all round; in times of spate these barbel will continue to feed and can be caught under the feet. However, a number of anglers prefer to meat fish out in the worst of the current. The strongest rig, and daftest I have seen to date, is to use a beachcaster and multiplying reel. It doesn't sound too bad so far, but a lump of folded sheet lead of up to 1lb is used. How on earth a bite is seen I just don't know. And how about a barbel or chub that hooks itself? Furthermore, where has the pleasure gone?

The author was presented with this terminal tackle used for flooded rivers. The wrapped sheet lead weighs 1lb 2oz. The feeder is for comparison.

6   Watercraft

A fisherman may have at his disposal all that is best in tackle. He may be fortunate also in having access to every top venue in the country, with lunchtime cocktails, high tea and a ghillie thrown in. Yet, if he has not learnt the art of watercraft, it is certain he will fail to be blessed with the true enjoyment of the sport.

Watercraft means many things: knowledge of nature, how to look at a river or lake, searching for signs which tell of fish – or lack of them – plus the knowledge of how a lake, river, or canal behave over varying weather conditions, also seasons, and time of day. Eventually, an angler will develop the instinct of how differing species of fish behave in the heat of summer, or depths of a freezing winter. The following chapters on the species can but assist with this knowledge, for only the individual can visit river or lake, looking for certain signs or indications, any of which may tell a tale. Should the angler be a novice, he can rest assured that watercraft will be learned by experience: decisions then become instinctive.

The vast majority of my river fishing has been on the Severn, Avon and Teme. As such, I have never needed to travel far to find good fishing, as these must be among the best rivers in the country. There are, of course, differences between a spate river, a chalk stream and a man-made drain. However, I do not consider that fish differ too much across the regions – a barbel is a barbel, a bream is a bream, etc. In the light of this, my beliefs on fish behaviour, location and habits are based on my findings while fishing these rivers. I am confident they can be applied to the various species elsewhere.

If there is one factor above all others in the angler's never-ending search for success, it is that of fish location; if he chucks his terminal rig to places where fish do not live, then he will find very little success. Should he have done his homework in finding the places where fish live, he must then present the rig in a manner which is acceptable to the species sought, using the most effective baits, at the best times, and with tackle balanced to that particular species.

It may be argued that the leger angler is limited to his choice of places to fish in that he fishes on the bottom. This may be so, but I don't know of any coarse fish which does not spend most of its life *feeding* on the bottom. It's not difficult to see the reason for this. Should everyone suddenly stop fishing, fish would continue to live quite happily, scoffing all forms of aquatic life, from insect larvae to water spiders, from weed to worm, all of which are found on the bed of a lake, river or canal.

The time at which the angler fishes is conducive also to his chances of success. By far, the vast majority of fishermen venture out in daytime, delighting in the warmth of a fine summer's day, intoxicated by the spread of

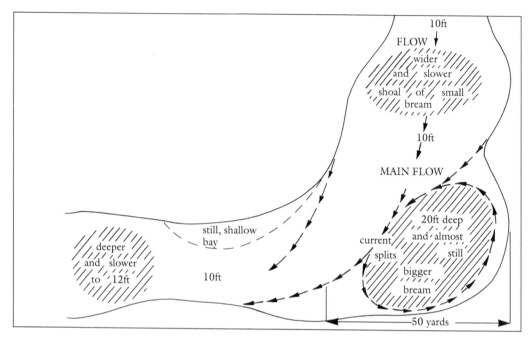

Fig. 5 A stretch of the Severn. Summer and early morning fishing.

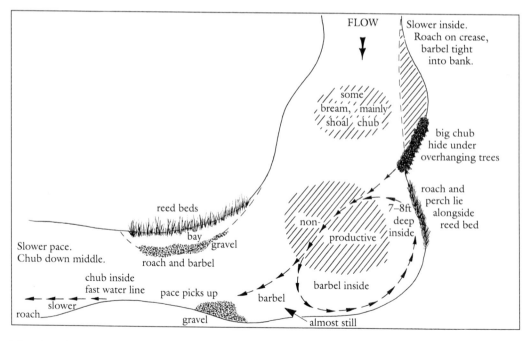

Fig. 6 The same stretch in winter and spring (normal level).

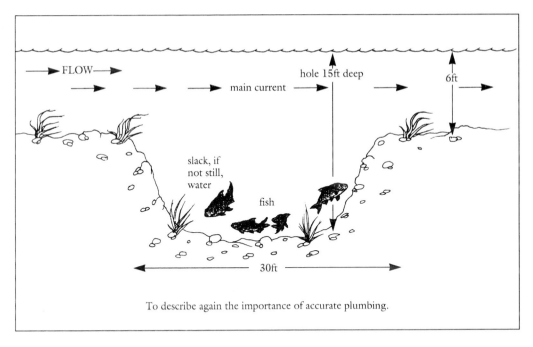

To describe again the importance of accurate plumbing.

Fig. 7 A typical middle Severn hole.

green meadow and grazing herds. The nocturnal angler, however, though he may be denied the visual pleasures of nature, will know his chances are increased tenfold by fishing during the hours of darkness.

Tench, carp, bream and eels, too, are species who feed better during early morning, late evening or throughout the night. To some extent this applies to *all* species, as any specimen hunter worth his floppy hat knows only too well. It may be that fish see better at night, or are by nature nocturnal, or even react to the effect of the moon as in a sea angler's solar chart. Whatever the real reasons – and I do not pretend to know them – I will not dwell on it too much when dealing with differing species. Suffice to say, and though I hate weight dropping, at 3 a.m. one morning in May 1988, on the wonderful Westwood Great Lake near my home in Droitwich, I caught a roach of 2lb 14oz which fell to four

lobworms on strong eel tackle. I cannot imagine that this could happen in the light of day.

Particular attention must be given to winter fishing. The most inexperienced of anglers realizes that above all other factors, water temperature plays a big part in fish location, and whether they will feed or not. The rough guide-line is 40°F, the lower limit at which fish feed freely, though the matchman, as usual, takes the whole matter further.

To mention once more the hallowed waters at Evesham, it was commonplace in the 1970s for anglers to telephone old Ernie Huxley, the then owner of the venue, to enquire the water temperature. They believed – quite rightly – that if the temperature was 39.6°F or above, roach could be caught, for roach stand colder water quite well. Chub needed just one degree more to feed, while below these levels there was just the possibility of the odd bite. This was the rule of thumb, a scale which many treated as a reason to venture out or stay warm in bed.

However, the whole thing must be taken further. If a water temperature has been below 39.0°F for a few days, and is on the rise when a reading is taken at 39+°F then fish will undoubtedly feed better than if the temperature is 40°F and falling. This applies to a large range of the lower temperatures. Certainly the best time to fish any winter river is after a spate, or long period of rain, when the colder water is washed out; while this is happening the temperature rises accordingly and fish feed with voracity. The same can be said of canal or lake, for rain is warmer than the ground waters during a hard winter.

The effect that atmospheric pressures have on the behaviour of fish is quite profound.

High or low pressure will determine if fish will feed or not, and for example, high pressure in late autumn or winter would be a good time to go fishing. In summer, however, this may mean in the middle of a heatwave, which is just about the worst time of all. On the other hand, high pressure on an overcast day will be very productive. In general terms, a cool day in summer, or the end of a warm period in winter, with little or no sun, and with a gentle breeze would be ideal conditions.

The many species of fish have further differing patterns of behaviour, taste and habitat. The following chapters cover the more popular species, and although many may *appear* similar in taste and habit, the seemingly unimportant quirks can make the difference between success and failure.

Twilight on Westwood Park. The angler knows that this time is the most productive of all.

7   Barbel

The biggest barbel I have seen was a magnificent fish of 16½lb caught on the Severn, from the weir at Holt Fleet in March 1986. The angler concerned, a quite venerable gentleman of indeterminable age, was fishing the tail end of the weir pool for salmon. We had stood talking for a few minutes, our voices loud over the roar of the water, during which he had cast his mounted prawn to the far side of the pool a couple of times, fishing with a sink-and-draw action. Without warning his twelve-foot rod arched over, the reel letting line as a fish ran.

After hooking the fish, and after playing it for a long time in the white rush of the weir, he, thinking he had been playing a salmon, became quite irate when a barbel surfaced. No serious salmon angler who may wait for years to catch his first, very expensive salmon, wants to see a barbel or any other coarse fish take his bait, no matter how big. The fact that he had caught what was obviously a record barbel meant little or nothing to the fellow.

The barbel floated belly-up in the slack of the margin. The prawn, tied to the strong salmon line of 15lb or so, hung from its mouth like a half sausage. Though fighting for many minutes, the fish had had no chance of escape on spinning tackle, and when finally netted remained very still – it had fought with every scrap of energy it possessed. Over three feet of solid bronze muscle, the barbel lay quietly in his massive landing-net as it was

weighed, after which we deducted the weight of the net. Oblivious to the roar of the weir, and fully aware this was a record barbel – one which every specialist barbel hunter in the country would give almost anything to catch – I settled the fish back into the river with its head upstream, stroking the broad muscular back and huge gills. At long last this beautiful barbel showed signs of recovery, the bronzed flanks hardening with renewed vigour, the gills opening further as the fish took in oxygen. Many minutes later, with a gentle swish of its broad tail, the barbel swam from my hands to safer climes.

These seven years later, I have no doubt that barbel approaching 20lb do live in the Severn; they may even be hooked on numerous occasions, though perhaps unknown to the angler. I recall my friend and Midlands match angler Charlie Hague spending the whole five hours of one match playing two fish. He failed to land either; in fact, he reckoned he didn't even manage to get them off the bottom.

For the last couple of years the stretch of the Severn below Worcester has been home to specimen hunters from all over the country. Cars arrive straight from office and factory, parked all night as these hardy folk search for that record barbel and the consequent fame that will go with it. How big this fish will be is irrelevant. But when it is captured – and I have no doubt it will be – the status quo will remain: the quest for a barbel just a few ounces more in weight will continue.

BAITS

The very first barbel I saw was lying on the bottom of the Hampshire Avon, under the footbridge which spans the Royalty stretch at Christchurch. I was fourteen years old at the time. Trembling with excitement, I set up a leger rig, put a lump of red-backed Edam cheese on the hook and lowered it to a spot one foot upstream from his massive head. He didn't budge. Lifting the rod, I allowed the cheese actually to bump his nose. Still there was no response. I changed the bait, using worm, bread and anything else which I thought the barbel might eat. Two weeks later, after completing my caravan holiday at Ringwood, the fish was still under the footbridge and for all I know he may still be there today. I have never forgotten this lesson. Barbel, perhaps more than any other fish, can be the most awkward to tempt when not in the mood to feed. If I knew then what I know now, I reckon I might have caught that wily old fish; though it would have taken planning and patience to do so.

Hempseed

Of all the attractors, hempseed remains at the top of the list for barbel. If you are using the swimfeeder, a few throws should be dedicated to putting a carpet of the seed on to the bottom, after which the feeder should be filled with a mixture of hemp and hookbait samples, perhaps sweetcorn, maggots or casters. When straight legering in an inside swim, a couple of pints can be thrown in for starters and then topped up at regular intervals; this should keep any foraging barbel from straying too far.

Hookbaits

Used in a swimfeeder, maggots must account for 95 per cent of all barbel caught, though these will not necessarily be big ones. Casters seem to work better when legered in the margins over a carpet of hempseed, and on the Severn this method produces fish to double figures.

A lobworm has always been a good bait for any big fish. Not too many years ago, the standard attack by Thames anglers was to pour thousands of worms into the river, following this with worm-bait terminal tackle; even today, barbel are taken regularly by salmon anglers who use bunches of lobworms. I do not advocate a whole bunch for barbel, but in winter, when a river may be heavily coloured, a big lob will be taken by many a fine fish.

Sweetcorn will always fool a fish or two, where a single or double grain on a size 14 hook has been the downfall of barbel over 10lb. Used over a carpet of hemp, corn is one of the best summer baits available.

Cheese has been a favourite of many barbel catchers for years, and the more smelly the cheese, the greater the chances of success. In cold water, cheese should be presented in paste form, kneaded with a bit of fresh bread to soften it to an edible consistency, though this is not the main reason for the softening. The idea is to allow the cheese to be soft enough for hook to be pulled out upon a strike, and so into a fish's mouth.

Luncheon meat, *the* prime bait for specimen barbel, is dealt with elsewhere.

LOCATION

I consider myself fortunate in having both the Severn and the Teme on my doorstep, for they are fine rivers of totally different character. The lower Severn is deep and steady, with barbel to be found just about everywhere, though at times they are so uncooperative that it may be thought there are none in the river.

To locate barbel on these deeper rivers is quite difficult, and the angler must be prepared for a great deal of searching. Above all, barbel prefer to bask over gravel beds, and if the angler knows of such places he will find barbel. If you know of what is loosely termed a 'bay' – a part of the river where the bank has been washed away – there is bound to be some gravel there or, at least, a stretch where the bed of the river is very stony. This will be the reason for the bank falling away, for it is much easier for the current to wash away earth full of stones than clay. The inside shallows may have a muddy bottom, but stones or gravel will be found off the outside edge.

In the low water of summer, the middle Severn is a continuation of shallows and streamer weed, and it is in this weed that the summer barbel live. At first glance it would seem difficult to fish such places, but a few minutes' careful study will reveal dark patches between the waving fronds; patches which mean clear runs. These runs can be safely fished with balanced leger tackle, but some knowledge of the form this weed takes is useful. I always liken streamer weed to bindweed, that nightmare of the gardener. A patch of bindweed on a garden may be feet across, yet if the weed is followed into the earth it is seen that one root of less than ⅛in diameter is causing all the trouble, the surface mass growing from this. Streamer weed is similar. The mass which appears on the surface is anchored to the bottom by very few roots, and it is under this roof that barbel live.

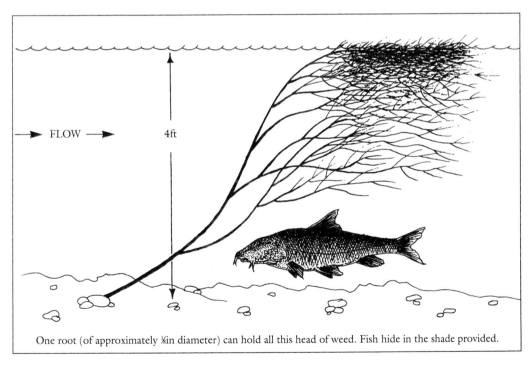

FLOW   4ft

One root (of approximately ⅛in diameter) can hold all this head of weed. Fish hide in the shade provided.

Fig. 8   A roof of *Ranunculus.*

If the angler simply wants to catch a netful of barbel, the feeder is without doubt the most effective method, when fished in lesser weeded areas. Though the fast centre of a ford looks very attractive, I have always found that the majority of barbel shoal to either side of this, out of the main flow but in a good position to dart in should any food be seen. This is easy feeder fishing, and when the angler has decided one side of the ford has been fished out, he can then transfer his attentions to the other; it is quite surprising how often this move can produce even more fish.

All the spate rivers that I know have holes in the bed, unseen to the angler, and these are places where barbel love to shelter. They can range in size from a small depression of one foot or so to a hole as big as a bomb crater, falling to over ten feet before returning to the normal depth once again. In a river with a high barbel population, these holes are quite literally stuffed with them, the reasons being that they are well out of the main current, and they are also places where water-borne food gathers naturally. Summer or winter, barbel do not stray too far from such havens. In general terms, therefore, always look for that part of a river with this difference.

From autumn through to spring – but excluding cold weather – I spend many days fishing exclusively for barbel. During these sessions I catch so many good roach that I now believe roach and barbel actually live together in complete harmony. At first I put this down to the hempseed which is so attractive to both species, yet I have lost count of the times that I have caught barbel and roach from the same swim without the use of hempseed. The main reason is, perhaps, that I do not fish too far out for barbel – or roach for that matter. The problems, of course, arise when I am roach fishing!

METHODS

The specialist angler, seeking his fish in more placid waters, will plan his attack based on days of pre-baiting with hempseed, throwing many pints each day into his selected swim. Barbel settle on this, following the aroma from far downstream, feeding confidently on the seed without interruption from leger or feeder. Come the day of reckoning, the angler will have increased his chances of success enormously. On big rivers such as the Severn I think barbel will take all the hempseed that can be thrown at them; they are virtually impossible to overfeed.

When much younger, and about to commence a match on the deeper Lower Severn with barbel as the main target fish, and after searching the swim for any possible snags, my common practice was to throw in at least four pints of hempseed in one go (I have been known to throw in a gallon). This does a number of things. The first is that every fish within twenty yards must run a mile; another is that a feeding area has been created, upon which the angler can concentrate his efforts. Should any barbel arrive in the vicinity, that is where they will stay. After a while – it may be half an hour or more – things begin to happen on the bed of the river. Barbel from downstream home in on the smell and begin to eat the seed, gently at first, building to a frenzy that at times will send masses of bubbles to the surface. A couple of good-sized barbel will mop up a big patch of hempseed in next to no time, and it takes no imagination to envisage even a gallon of hemp disappearing very quickly. As they sup this carpet of seed, samples of hookbait such as casters, sweetcorn or maggots are introduced, a few at a time, enough for the fish to look upon them as something special. They then become selective, taking the hookbaits before the seed, licking the icing off the cake.

There can, however, be no doubt that 99 per cent of specimen barbel caught are taken on meat. I cannot bring myself to delve into the supposed latent intelligence of the barbel which, it would appear to some anglers, scoff meat as it contains protein and is therefore nutritious and body-building. I believe barbel eat meat because they like it – and for no other reason. Most anglers will know just how effective a cube of luncheon meat can be when fishing for barbel or chub, yet time and time again I hear of anglers who have difficulty in keeping the meat on the hook. I have heard so many tales of this problem, and the many ways in which to combat it, that I have made a study of the whole thing. My conclusions are that most problems originate with the cast.

Meat is soft and with any bait which is soft, be it paste, worms or wasp grub, a jerky cast will send it flying away at any tangent. The cast must be an acceleration, starting slowly, then moving quickly through the motion, thus removing any jerk which could pull the hook through the bait. Furthermore, instead of preparing a tinful of cubes, you will find it much better to take the meat from a tin and cut off a slice ½in thick. Tear out a piece the size of a middle fingernail, then thread it up the line, followed by a second piece which sits on the hook, after which the first lump is pulled down to rest on the other. This will greatly reduce the possibility of the meat coming off the hook, and I will guarantee that if meat is on the hook when it hits the water, that is where it will stay. But a more important factor now emerges.

A cube is edible and will catch fish. However, the rough edges of the two-piece

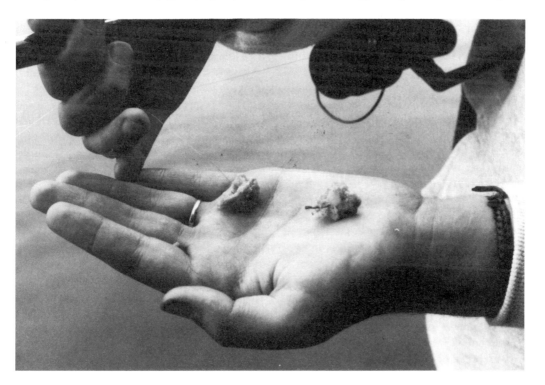

Two rough pieces of meat are much better than a cube.

method will allow tiny pieces of meat to be washed away, so creating a line of morsels which flow down with the current – a natural form of groundbait. Fish follow this to the source, and if the angler casts to the same spot each time it is possible to shoal fish, keeping them in one spot for a length of time. Eventually, as bites are missed – which they surely will be – the fish fall downstream, following the bits of meat regurgitated by scared or hooked fish. I can find no way in which to prevent this happening, all I can suggest is to capitalize upon the initial bite rate, after which it may be prudent to try a completely different line of attack.

A practice all too common is to use a piece of matchstick or strong weed, inserted under the meat at the bend of the hook to keep it in place. This does very well but it also inhibits hook penetration. When a fish takes a piece of meat, the resulting strike should pull the hook through the meat and into the mouth of the fish. Any bit of matchstick, reed or anything else will prevent the hook from coming out of the meat and it then acts as a buffer, bouncing against the mouth of the fish. This is even more prevalent when the water is cold and the meat tends to be more solid.

Size of hook will vary from a 10 when things are difficult, and when everything needs to be scaled down, to a size 2 or larger when the barbel are bent on hara-kiri, in which case the whole of the rig balance needs to be stepped. A reel line of 6.1lb is strong enough for any barbel, to which an eyed hook can be tied direct, using the whipping knot. A knot I use for attaching the lead-link has no name, and as so many things in fishing, it simply happened. This is the sliding knot, one which has never let me down.

The line for the lead-link should be of weaker breaking strain; should the lead be snagged it will be the only loss. Before attaching the lead-link, form a multi-turn water loop at the point in the reel line where you decide to put the lead-link, which should be half the distance of the hooklength. This is the 'stopper' – the point at which the link will stop. There are no beads, leger stops, swivels or other encumbrances to complicate the terminal tackle, with the only possible weak spot at the water loop. If enough turns are given, even this will be minimal.

Feedering for Barbel

The feeder continues to be the most widely used method for the shoal barbel on rivers which contain this fine fish. The requirements of rod and reel have been covered in detail in Chapter 1, where a strong quiver-tip rod of a through action is required, capable of not only casting a 4oz feeder, but of winding it back in with a possible double-figure barbel on the hook.

The robust open-face reel must be loaded with line of no less than 6lb b/s, which should be checked regularly for wear, for the constant abrasions caused by an innocent bank of weed are surprisingly bad, as is the wear caused by bedrock, with which spate rivers are blessed. There is no need to go to fine extremes with the hooklength: 2.6lb is ample to commence with, though as the day progresses this can be increased if fish are suicidal. To repeat: everything should be balanced with all factors taken into consideration.

Terminal rigs for barbel should be kept simple. I have no doubt that more fish are lost, and more bites are missed, as a result of over-complicated terminal tackles. When attaching the swivels it is important to tuck the half-blood knot at each point to eliminate any possibility of it slipping, which can be a common occurrence with softer nylon lines. Length of feeder-link is not too critical, despite what a lot of anglers will tell you. Most feeders are sold with a link of just a few inches, and variations in the distance of this link is, in most cases, unnecessary. The hooklength should be of around 2ft, shortening this if bites are missed, until the hookbait lies right alongside the feeder.

Although hooks are a personal matter, feeder fishing for barbel demands a strong hook, and none comes stronger than a Drennan Carbon Feeder. When using either maggot or caster as bait, a size 20 may be needed in hard times, but generally speaking, a size 16 or 18 will suffice on most occasions. One important factor regarding hooks is that when fishing a river with a hard rock or gravel bottom, the hook needs to be inspected regularly for damage. Even the hardest or sharpest of hooks will lose its point if dragged into a lump of rock. Whatever his choice, the *really* keen

angler will file down the spade on all of his hooks to alleviate the possibility of tangle on retrieve, when the hook spins against the push of water on the spade. In my experience, a swivel does little to prevent this.

Balance must again be mentioned in selection of the feeder, for the correct choice of weight can result in a netful; get it wrong and you may see just a few lucky fish. The ideal is to study the water for a few moments, assessing the depth, current, etc. until you decide which feeder weight is most likely to hold bottom when full. The first cast will determine how accurate you were. If the feeder goes to the bottom like a ton weight and stays there until it is reeled in, then it is too heavy. If it bounces along the bed immediately, then it's too light. Trim weights are added or

Barbel fishing on the lower Severn. The fish are so big that the gunman stands by.

deducted until the feeder stays put for a few minutes while the feed washes out. Then a small lift of the rod allows it to move downstream a little before settling once more. This is perfect balance – any movement apart from this can be treated as a bite.

The instinct to tighten into a feeder is asking for trouble, and the need to fish with a loose line is vital. Even a small barbel will take the hookbait with venom, where to break a 2.6lb hooklength is all too easy. After the feeder has settled, let a few feet of line off the spool, allowing it to form a bow downstream. Various rigs have been invented for this type of fishing, using loops which allow the feeder to slide up and down, thus allowing fish to feel less resistance. While this may be so in theory, it is wise not to complicate your fishing by using rigs which may be sometimes unnecessary.

Now we must look for two types of bite. One, the more usual kind, is to see the bow lengthen as the feeder is moved, resulting in the tip straightening. This should be struck at immediately, lifting the rod well back over the shoulder, though care must be taken should the fish be running away from the fishing position. The second type of bite is to see the bow tightening as a fish takes line through the swivel, where the feeder may be held with weed. All too often, the fish will hook itself. The angler, therefore, must show even greater care with this type of bite, for it all happens quite quickly and fast reactions are needed. The reel, if set correctly, will give line before it reaches breaking point, but only if it has a cushion of time.

Straight Legering

This is my favourite way of catching deep-water barbel, those big old 'uns who retire to easier climes, and who have enough experience of the feeder to keep well away.

The first thing to do is to establish that the swim has no major snags. These may be visible, such as trees which have fallen into the water, or sunken boats, or they may be more difficult to locate, for instance, a bankside tree may send bare roots out into the river. A few casts with a heavy lead will soon pick out anything to worry about, and if proved too difficult, the angler should choose another swim.

After using all sorts of rods, from a twelve-foot float rod to a longer than usual light feeder rod, I have found a medium-action quiver tip of about ten feet in length to be ideal. The tip should be delicate enough to register the bite, for when supping particle baits such as maggots and hempseed, barbel do not move very far between mouthfuls. The tip, therefore, must be fine enough to show the initial tremble, tapering quickly to take part in the action of the rod under power.

As this method is used for near-bank fishing, there is no need for complicated tackles. Using a reel line of 3.2lb direct to the hook, I simply tie on a lead-link of 2.6lb, using the sliding knot (see page 19), which is stopped at the point the angler wishes by a multi-turn water knot. As this is a small bait method, the hook I can recommend is the Drennan Forged Match, using size 14 for a bunch of casters, down to a size 18 with a single caster if things prove to be tough going. The hooklength needs to be about 2ft or more, giving the fish time to pick up the bait without being alarmed, yet it is very rare to hook a barbel at the back of the mouth. In fact, there have been many times when I have landed barbel with the hook stuck in the barbule, such can be the delicacy of their feeding habits. If you catch one or two fish, and no further bites are forthcoming, a single maggot to a size 18 hook will sometimes produce further bites, with bronze being the favoured colour.

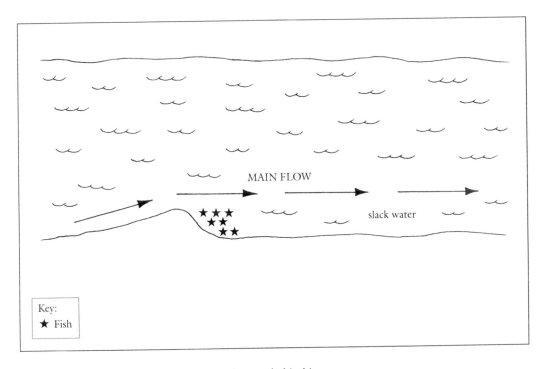

Fig. 9 Mid-river contour. Fish lie in slack water behind it.

The crease of the current – the joining of the slow inside and faster main current – is the spot to aim for. Commencing with a double caster to a size 16 hook, cast the terminal tackle into the main stream and allow it to be carried in the slower part of the swim, settling where it leaves the heavier flow. Hempseed should now be introduced at the top of the swim, say a pint to start with, topped up until signs are noticed that fish have arrived. This can be where a barbel may show itself by rolling at the bottom of the

A barbel bay at Holt Fleet. This is covered with gravel, and is also the home of big roach in winter.

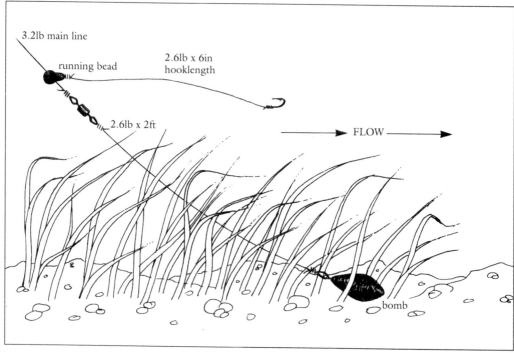

Fig. 10 Simple rig for running water with bottom weed.

swim or, more usually, where a mass of bubbles are sent to the surface, a sure sign that barbel are vacuuming up the hempseed. Throw in casters upstream of the hempseed as they will sink much more slowly, with the idea being to get them to reach the bottom at the same spot as the hempseed. Should the swim be really deep, where loose feeding is thought to be guesswork, the same baiting programme can be carried out with a bait dropper. This is an item of tackle which is attached to the line by the hook, filled with whatever bait is desired, and lowered to the bed. Once contact is made, the release is activated and the bait pours out. It is simple and very

Bait droppers. When the dropper hits the bottom the lid is released.

effective, as most things should be in any form of angling.

When a barbel takes the bait, there is nothing left to doubt. After perhaps a tiny tremble or two, as the fish uses its barbules to taste, the tip arcs round and the angler must be prepared to give line off the reel instantly, until he has guessed what size the fish may be. A barbel will, at most times anyway, tear off upstream and out into the middle of the river. This is fine for the angler as it gives him a chance to estimate the size of the fish while it is in a position where he can do something about his next move. If he is into a small one of up to 6lb or so, it's a simple matter of the normal pump and reel in action, taking care not to create any jerking movements which could disturb the hook hold.

If the rod continues to bend each time the angler attempts to stop his fish, and the fish takes on the appearance of a Polaris submarine, then the whole picture changes. It is now a matter of tiring the barbel, which is, give or take a snag or two, not too difficult. As long as there is deep water in front of the angler, the fish will come to the net quite easily, though if there is a shallow inside shelf, a long landing net can be useful; to encourage a big barbel to swim on to this shelf is just about impossible. If the barbel comes to the net upright, it is unlikely that the angler will be able to net it, for it will still be full of fight. The best time to net a big barbel is when it comes in belly-up – a fish which has given everything it had in the way of a fight. To hold a good-sized barbel is to marvel at the hardness of the muscle, the very spirit of the fish.

It's a grand way to catch barbel. I would, however, implore the reader that once he has landed a good fish, and has taken his photographs, he should place the fish in the water, taking time to stroke it back to strength before letting it swim away. Any fish which fights as hard as the barbel deserves such affection.

BARBEL IN SUMMER

Barbel in a summer or autumn river, a river perhaps full of streamer weed, hide under the fronds and in the clearer, slightly deeper runs between banks of ranunculus. To cast to these positions demands no great skill: once the distance is gauged it is a matter of constant casting to get some bait in the swim to attract fish, and of keeping enough going in to keep them there. Maggot or casters are equally attractive to barbel, but copious amounts of hempseed must also go in. The cast is made to a dark patch between weed beds, where the feeder is stopped in mid-flight, entering the water with a fearful wallop. On the Severn, this wallop is quite important, for Severn barbel now associate this noise with food.

There is a school of thought which believes barbel line up for their food, taking a morsel before tearing away to the back of the queue upstream, awaiting their turn once more. It's all very nice and civilized to imagine fish behaving like this, but believe me, neither barbel nor any other species is that cute. What happens is they grab the food, flicking away before any other fish can see it. Then back they come for more, but must shove through any other fish to get there. When they feel the hookbait, and when the resistance of hook or swimfeeder is felt, the hook goes home and off goes the fish, frightened to death at being hooked. If the angler is careful in keeping the hooked fish away from the feeding area, the remainder of the shoal will continue to feed confidently once more. Having studied barbel for many years, and having watched them feed over hemp, caster and/or meat, I have yet to see them form a queue.

WINTER BARBEL

Ask any barbel specialist which conditions he prefers in the hunt for his fish, and you may be very surprised. He will paint his dream picture of a river high with floodwater, of a thick murky colour, when only the totally dedicated angler ventures forth. Furthermore, he will prefer to fish at night. These efforts are well worth making, for the winter barbel is a different fish from the summer – and different also depending on the time of day.

It's not difficult to see why this is so. In the clearness of a summer river, barbel or any other fish *see* their food, being instinctively suspicious of a bait anchored to a piece of line, behaving strangely in a moving current. At night-time, however, fish can feed only by smell, homing in to the source which it will attempt to eat – and I choose that word deliberately as at night, fish have no time for tasting or sampling.

Two main baits come to mind for winter barbel: meat and lobworm. Due to lower water temperatures, meat is best presented in paste form as this will remain soft, giving a better chance of the hook making penetration. The worm almost speaks for itself: a lobworm hooked in the centre with a size 8 hook will tempt any barbel within twenty yards.

The bite from a barbel at night is almost always quite savage and without any preamble; the rod end simply bends very fast. This activity can be used to advantage by the angler for it gives him the opportunity to strengthen his tackle accordingly; line strength can be increased, as can bait and hook size. The opportunity to have a close look at the mouth of a big barbel is not to be missed, for it will be seen just how big a bait

Touch-legering hand positions.

The author's son Steve with a barbel of 9lb 4oz caught in a water temperature of 3°C.

Hard at work. Fishing for barbel at the neck of Lax Lane ford below Bewdley.

John Sidley with a 6lb 3oz eel from Westwood Park.

Snow time on the frozen tiny River Salwarpe in Worcestershire.

Three barbel for 18lb and 10lb of nice roach. A good match win.

A flooded Severn below Worcester Bridge. Fish can be caught, barbel in particular, but the angler is very limited in his choice of methods. Meat or worm are really the only practical baits.

Feeder fishing the far side of the Severn below Bewdley. The rod is
mounted high to keep as much line as possible out of the water.

The two anglers are fishing a 6ft deep steady run. Sixty feet below, the river deepens to over 15ft before rising to 6ft once more.

Find a raft like this and you will have found chub, a fish that delights in having a roof over its head.

Steve with a common carp. He hooked this fish as it touched the keepnet in less than one foot of water.

Islands above Arley on the Severn. The deep cleft between the shallows on either side holds big chub, easy to fish for with a straight leger rig. A swimfeeder would require too much lead to hold bottom.

A man at peace. The Severn below Bewdley Bridge.

A deep hole in the Terne. Double-figure fish have been caught from here, but it needs good angling to bring them to the net.

Eric Smith with a lone roach caught on a piece of breadflake. It was the result of one bite during a period when the river was below 3°C.

A roach angler using hemp and tares along the edge of the reed mace bed. A typically good swim for summer roach.

he can take in, where a knob of paste on a size 2 hook is certainly not too big.

There is no doubt that touch-legering is the better method for single bait fishing, more so at night when human senses undergo change. The explanations contained in Chapter 5 are useful, but at night it's best to fish with the rod pointed directly at the leger. I am no great believer in touch legering with loose line, for far from being a looser presentation, there can be no doubt that line which is bowed creates resistance upon the strike, which is akin to pulling line around a barrel. Far better to be in direct contact with the hookbait when instinct will be the best bite indicator you can find, especially at night. Tiny plucks in the line can be felt instantly, though they must be left until a definite take occurs, with the line pulling firmly, or jerking through the fingers. The strike must then be a firm fluid movement, up and over the shoulder, until contact is made. The more relaxed specimen hunter may use a Betalight, a small diode which glows in the dark, and can be attached to the rod tip without fouling the line. When the tip dips with a bite, so does the bulb, but beware of overhanging trees or the bulb will end up like a fairy light.

Believe me, touch-legering, though requiring great concentration, is very exhilarating.

SMALL-RIVER BARBEL

Far from the predictability of the Severn, the Teme is a small river which can vary from an inches-deep rapid to a twenty-foot deep hole within a matter of yards, changing direction again and again as it meanders through the hop fields of the fertile Teme valley. Any effluent which goes into the river is minimal and of an agricultural nature. As such, the behaviour of fish – and in particular barbel – differs greatly from those of the Severn.

Whereas the feeding pattern of a Severn barbel can at times be no more than a couple of taps, the Teme counterpart will take the rod off the rest. Also, to heave masses of hempseed into a small river is to send barbel shooting off in all directions; they much prefer a single large bait.

I have heard this behaviour is similar to other barbel rivers which are on the small side. The fact that Teme barbel are restricted to narrow banks and a much clearer, shallower river, could mean that no matter where they feed, snags are usually in sight, and it needs only a flick of a broad tail to find sanctuary. These smaller rivers have differing visible features, such as sharp bends, deep holes against high banks, and greater tree cover. Barbel can be found at any of these features, and they will live between banks of weed, at the end of fast fords, under the sill of a weirpool, and in fact anywhere which shows character.

Rivers which vary in character and depth give barbel the chance to select their habitat, and I have always believed that the bigger fish (those over 8lb) prefer the quieter side of life, seeking the more placid, deeper type of waters. Those barbel of the Hampshire Avon, Kennet, Wensum, and so on have little choice, for those excellent barbel rivers are much of a muchness in depth and flow, ultra-clean streams where the fish are found hidden amongst thick streamer weed.

On a river with a high barbel population, such as the Teme or Severn, no matter where an angler may fish he will be within casting distance of barbel. Many anglers create problems for themselves by casting too far for these fish, for more barbel live close to the bank than anywhere else. This behaviour is even more prevalent with fish of a specimen size who can be found virtually under the bankside vegetation itself, using tree or bush as cover.

Big barbel are big because they are not stupid. However, they do not carry a ruler or

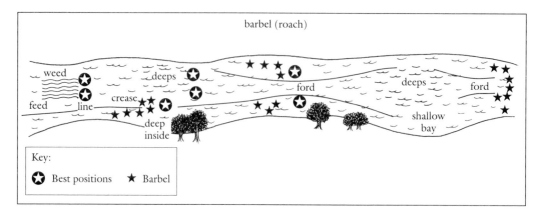

Fig. 11 Typical middle Severn variations.

micrometer around with them, nor do they mind if the hookbait is hard on the bottom, or an inch off it. What they *do* like is a hookbait which is static. Like any other living creature, they develop habits to find food as easily as they possibly can without expending too much energy. Once the younger, more playful days are over, the old 'uns prefer a quiet life, spending their days under the lee of a bank, far from the heavy currents of winter, away from the wash of summer boat traffic. Food is plentiful, for the bank is where people throw bread for ducks, where worms wash out of banks and where caterpillars drop from trees. Make no mistake: big barbel are bone idle – until they are hooked.

A narrow neck of the river Teme. To catch double-figure barbel here is not uncommon – but adequate tackle must be used!

8   Bream

Bream are possibly the most sought-after fish we have in these isles. There are two distinct species: the silver bream found in the eastern part of the country, which grows to no more than a pound or two, and the more well-known common, or bronze, bream which will grow to over fifteen pounds. Though not the hardest of fighters, the bigger of the species gives rise to enough interest to make the hunt worth the effort. The term 'big' is relative for, as with all fish, the size of a specimen will depend on the habitat. A river bream of 6lb will excite most anglers, but a specimen from a Cheshire mere will need to be over 10lb to raise an eyebrow.

BAITS

Not too many years ago, before barbel ruled the Severn, bream were the main target on the lower river. With matches of over 500 pegs, the pot was well worth winning, resulting in anglers from all over the country attending. Outsiders came with the idea of the caster/worm cocktail being the answer to it all when, in fact, Severn bream rarely responded to worm at any time. Gozzer was the prime bait, with breadflake a close second, and though just a few bream were caught on worm, the angler was more likely to hook undersized eels. However, on bream rivers such as the Witham or Welland, rivers with an equally large head of eels, worm is the main

bait and has been for years. Yet it should always be remembered that the bream is a fish which responds to most popular baits, with redworms, red-dyed maggots, casters, gozzers and bread being the favourites. The lesson here must be to keep an open mind. Depending on the venue, and which bait anglers on that venue use week in and week out, one will be predominant.

Bait requirements for a day out breaming could go something like the following: a gallon of dry crumb, four pints of casters, two pints of squatts, half a loaf of new-sliced bread, a quantity of red maggots, some lobs and a carton of redworms. A couple of tins of sweetcorn would not go amiss, and if the

Cocktail of breadflake and single maggot.

This 3lb bream swallowed two squatts on size 22 hook at 40 yards, using 1lb hooklength.

attractor, an enticing cloud which will excite fish into feeding. A bream angler can put so much groundbait into a swim, that should it indeed be eaten as solid food, a shoal of any size would be stuffed to inertia in next to no time.

As a past matchman, a breed who always look for the edge, I find commercial groundbait lacking in many ways. It lacks freshness, and the thicker grains of the coarse variety will feed fish too much. It can also vary immensely in ingredients. What may appear to be simple ground brown bread, or pure white crumb may contain all sorts of rubbish, leaving a well-mixed bowl of groundbait like a lump of drying concrete. There is nothing you can do with this type of stuff; better to feed it to the ducks and have words with your supplier.

The finest groundbait available can be made at home. First obtain a few stale loaves (at a cheap price) and, after removing the crust, allow it to soak overnight. Place a colander in a large bowl, then press the soaked bread through it. Fill the bowl with water, and a scum will appear on the surface. This should be poured away, after which the process is repeated until the water is clear. Then, by squeezing the remaining mess in a cotton bag, most of the water will be removed; the result is a pure white groundbait. If this is not quite stiff enough, a small amount of fine, white crumb can be added, but only as a last resort. I can assure the reader that this will be a far superior groundbait to any which can be purchased.

Groundbait additives are personal. Again, I must confess that I have reservations regarding the effectiveness of many of these attractors, yet if a man thinks a particular brand is effective, and doesn't feel confident without it, then he would be daft not to use it (as long as he can afford it – the price of some is prohibitive). Personally, I believe angling ability is far more important.

angler is ultra-keen and has an understanding wife, mother and neighbours, he should have a tin of treasured gozzers.

I have always been of the opinion that big fish prefer big baits, and specimen bream are no exception. The big lobworm approach will catch more specimen bream than anything else, but it is a method which can be long in the wait, resulting in just a single fish here and there.

Groundbaiting

Although there is no doubt that bream do eat groundbait, at no time must groundbait be considered fish-food. In basic form it is a carrier of food, be it maggots, casters, or any other form of particle feed. It is also an

Selection of the more popular groundbait additives.

If commercial crumb is used, it must be mixed well before actually fishing. It is advisable to mix enough to last perhaps an hour, as the consistency of groundbait changes as time passes, where the adding of water does nothing to improve it; far better to make a new mix. If feeder methods are used, standard brown crumb will suffice, having enough adhesion to hold in the open-end feeder. If, however, the groundbait is catapulted or thrown by hand, then an 80/20 per cent white mix will hold together much better, preventing the ball from breaking in mid-air. Also, in deeper water, it will hold together long enough for the ball to reach the bottom.

Using either a proprietary groundbait bowl or a shallow container, put a small amount of water in first, adding the groundbait bit by bit, until the required consistency is obtained.

Even then, leave it for a few minutes before checking again, adding water or groundbait as required. A shoal of bream needs something more than groundbait to keep it in a swim, and by far the best magnet is casters; squatts, too, will keep them grubbing about without over-feeding them. A handful of casters is added to the groundbait and mixed well, though kept in one corner which is free of other ground-bait; any greater amount of casters could become floaters if the day is sunny, rising in the water and taking the fish up with them. During the course of a session, say six hours, four pints of casters would certainly not be too much for a good shoal of bream. A few squatts can be added, just enough to keep some form of activity to interest the shoal. Should casters be unavailable, a couple of pints of maggots can be scalded, which will kill them stone

Filling an open-end feeder with one hand. Note casters in one corner.

STILLWATER BREAM

The first thing to do is to get rid of this word stillwater, for there is no such thing. Every lake, gravel pit or pool I have fished has, at some time during the day, shown movement of one kind or another.

Large reservoirs are initially formed by damming a stream or river within a valley, where the water level reaches wherever the planners have agreed upon. These feeder streams have a continuous effect in creating what is sometimes a very strong current, and when in spate this will be increased, as will the colour, though this will take time to swill around the water mass. When lakes take on this colour, fish, especially bream, react accordingly and are known to go on a real feeding beano.

dead, thus preventing them from crawling into gravel or debris on the bed.

Pre-baiting

The angler who has time to visit a swim daily to bait up in readiness for an assault will greatly increase his chances of success. This pre-baiting programme can be carried out over a few days or even a week or two – the longer the better. There are no great secrets to this; it's a simple matter of putting in large amounts of groundbait and particle baits – maggots, casters, sweetcorn – anything, in fact, which bream will take as hookbait. Another advantage of this method is that on stillwater venues where bream travel set paths, the time can be noted when they arrive in the baited swim and mop up the free feed. It is surprising how accurate this period will be, and you can virtually set the time daily that bream visit the swim. The benefit lies in that once the angler has caught fish from the swim on two or three occasions, he will be aware of the feeding times and can plan ahead accordingly.

Wind, of course, plays a major part in the movement of stillwater. A good breeze creates conflicting underwater currents, with the surface area taking on the appearance of a slow river, yet two feet under this, the current may be going in exactly the opposite direction. Even on a still, windless day, I have found that stillwaters can move considerably, with the direction of current changing without apparent reason. To go into this in depth would require a deep knowledge of science, a subject with which I am unfamiliar; suffice it to say that it does happen, and the angler should be prepared.

A good way to find out just what is happening underwater is to mix some groundbait that is just damp, kneading a lump quite hard before throwing it in close enough to the bank to be seen. Once on the bottom it will

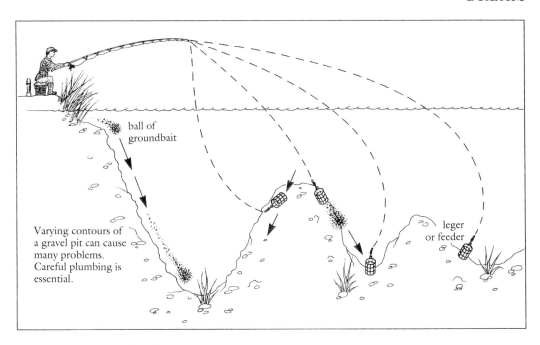

ball of
groundbait

Varying contours of
a gravel pit can cause
many problems.
Careful plumbing is
essential.

leger
or feeder

Fig. 12 Typical gravel-pit bottom.

begin to break up, sending tiny particles to the surface which will be directed by the current, giving a positive indication of flow and pace. Another method is to cast a leger, or feeder, letting line off the reel to observe which way the bow will form. This knowledge of current is all-important, for it is of little use putting out groundbait in one spot if it flows to settle at a point ten yards from the hook-bait.

Anyone who has first-hand knowledge of large bream catches will know just how much groundbait is needed to keep bream interested. As a consequence of this, some anglers throw in as much groundbait as is possible, which, at certain times, can be very effective. However, thought must be given to what happens underwater. The practice of throwing or catapulting ball after ball of groundbait on to the same spot should be avoided at all costs, for a bream shoal can be as big as a herd

of Australian sheep, running into hundreds, and will not take kindly to a pile of ground-bait four feet high and two feet across. They much prefer to find a grazing ground where they can move around at will, and it is quite obvious that a good-sized shoal will cover a large area. A few balls scattered around a three-square-yard patch will keep a shoal interested much longer than putting twice the amount all in one spot.

To throw by hand to the same area constantly is simply a matter of practice, but the use of a catapult needs more thought. The choice of cup must be of the stiff moulded type which retains its shape when pulled. A handful of groundbait is squeezed and rolled into a ball shape, after which it should be dipped into water, glazing it to a non-stick surface, and placed into the cup. With the arm holding the catapult frame at full stretch, the cup is pulled back and released, upon which the frame hand

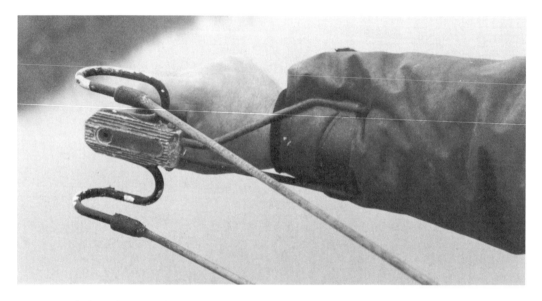

For extremely long distances this version of a sporting catapult can be used.

Catapulting to distance. Note large cup for ground bait. Hands should occupy
the same positions each time for accuracy.

must be dropped quickly, a form of slinging action. If both hands are at the same places at each time of release, and if each ball is of a similar size, then it follows that every one will arrive at near enough the same spot every time. (To use live maggots larger than squatts will make the ball of groundbait break up in mid-air.) Should the angler have access to a boat, he may find it better to carry out the initial baiting by rowing out and quietly dropping large quantities of groundbait into the swim. Groundbait in this situation could comprise normal bread crumb, plus any amount of sweetcorn, casters, worms, bits of bread – anything which may be later used as hookbait. If the chosen swim is far away, the area can be marked with a brightly coloured bulky float tied to a length of line tied to a stone. After plumbing the depth, the float is fixed in the cocked position, which will give positive sighting from the bank. When the session is over, a leger cast across the line will soon retrieve the marker rig.

Location

Stillwater bream are much easier to locate than their river counterparts – they go where the food is. Beds of natural food, such as bloodworm, can be discovered by studying the surface of a pond or lake. Choose a still, warm evening, and watch for swallows and swifts as they dip to the surface, picking off hatching flies or egg-laying duns. In the case of a natural lake this could be anywhere, though usually over water of moderate depth. In a gravel pit, the situation changes in that the silt beds where natural food thrive will be found only in those areas of the pit which have a flat bottom; this is where you will find bloodworm beds – and bream shoals sometimes numbering hundreds.

Before starting to fish, make sure the area chosen is flat enough to be muddy. The many

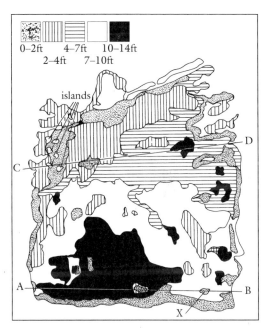

Fig. 13 Soundings of Upton Warren gravel pit.

slopes of a gravel pit make it difficult for food to congregate, or for silt to settle, and is just about impossible to feed correctly, for a ball of groundbait will simply roll downhill to the flat part. This applies to a feeder or Arlesey bomb if they are inadvertently cast to the far side of an underwater valley. In this case, they roll towards the angler, though it may take a little time for this to happen. Occasionally, a terminal rig cast to such a position may settle without moving for a short period. If any current is in evidence, it will eventually take the slack out of the line and finally move the rig; this could result in the angler reading the straightening of the tip as a drop-back bite, with the consequent strike sending bait everywhere. I cannot overstress the importance of diligent plumbing in a gravel pit. Apart from the foregoing observations, should the water be used for another activity such as sailing, then someone, somewhere,

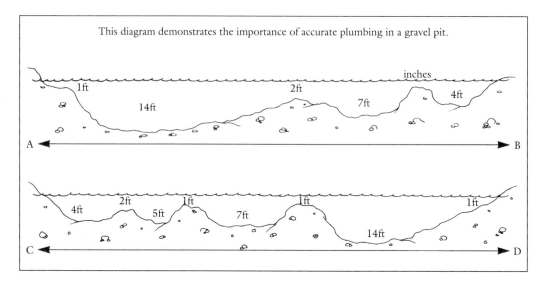

Fig. 14 Cross-section of gravel pit shown on previous page.

will have access to a chart which will show shallows and deeps.

One thing you can be sure of is that bream do not take kindly to weeded areas. They are a cumbersome fish, and have enough difficulty in searching around for food while standing on their heads, without the added problems of thick weed. The angler can eliminate these areas with confidence.

Come late evening, that magical time when the world of the fisherman takes on new meaning, stillwater bream begin to wander around, and are known to have a regular beat which they constantly patrol. Should a lake be clear, and shallow enough, the path of nomadic bream shoals can be spotted by detecting the areas of water which cloud over as the shoal dig up the bed, searching for aquatic life on which to feed. They also roll on the surface, which though a method of location is, in my experience, not a sure sign that they are feeding. I have found the reverse to be true, for I have never caught bream by casting to the roll.

Though bream of five to six pounds are found in shoals of good size, the real bonzos over ten pounds are loners, or swim in shoals of just two or three fish. The hours of darkness are without doubt the best times to fish for big bream, and though the approach and methods are similar, thought must be given to bite indication. Optonics and bobbins are commonly used, but care must be taken to ignore the bleeps caused by liners, where the bobbin shoots up – and down just as fast. When it rises, and the tip starts to go round, that will be a fish.

Feeder Fishing

The set-up of a feeder rig for stillwater bream is simplicity itself. A reel line of 2.6lb is adequate, though for really long-distance casting it's wise to increase this to 3.2lb, for to hook a shy-biting fish at sixty yards requires a long strike; if the line is too fine it may stretch against the weight of the feeder without putting the hook home. For the normal run of bream up to 5lb, the hooklength need not be more than 2.1lb, though a matchman will go finer than this at times. Many successful match anglers regularly catch winning nets of bream using size 22 hooks to 1.1lb hooklength, swearing that this not only increases the bite rate but also results in bigger fish. There can be no argument that finer lines and smaller hooks will result in more bites, but such a fine approach is for the experienced angler only.

A cage-type feeder is a good choice as it has the least resistance on the retrieve, and can be attached to the main line by bead or swivel; either way, do keep it all simple. Stillwater bream do not dash off into the far regions, and do not rock and roll enough to warrant a complex set-up of swivels, beads, anti-tangle rigs and other daft ideas. The feeder link need not be more than 6in, while the tail, or hooklength, should be of around 2ft, but be prepared to lengthen this if bites fail to develop. On such occasions, when the fish only play around with the hookbait, that extra length will sometimes make them bold enough to take it with confidence.

The mouth of a bream is tender and soft, therefore the choice of hook pattern is of prime importance. The great bream anglers I

have known, whether match or specimen hunters, have always settled for the forged variety as the wire is thicker, whereas a crystalbend fine-wire hook has a nasty habit of 'cheese-cutting' through the mouth of a bream. One of my favourites when using maggot or casters is the Drennan Super Spade, a round-bend forged reversed pattern which once in the mouth of a bream does not come out.

Before starting to fish, I like to put in a few balls of groundbait squeezed solid enough to reach the bottom, backing this up with the feeder as the day progresses. Three or four balls containing hookbait samples are ample, and this should be the only time loose groundbait is called for. To put in more heavy balls when a shoal is on the feed is asking for trouble, as bream that are feeding in earnest don't like to be bombarded from above.

It's wise to attach the hookbait before filling the feeder, as any small, accidental knock may result in groundbait falling out. As casters are in the groundbait, the first hook-

As bream do not run with a bait, any encumbrance such as swivels are unnecessary.

2–3lb main line

water loop knot

loop to loop

1–2ft

open end feeder

1–2lb hooklength

Fig. 15 Simple rig for stillwater bream.

bait should be a couple of them impaled on a size 16 hook. In my experience, a light-coloured caster is best for bream – why I don't know, but then I'm not a bream!

Drop the feeder into the groundbait bowl, and while covering one end with a thumb, press a groundbait/caster mix into the other end, compacting it to the degree where you sense it will hold there until reaching the bottom. I cannot overstress the importance of this, for groundbait which falls from the feeder at mid-water does a number of things. Fish will rise to the cloud, searching around for loose feed and, also, should there be any current, the cloud will wash downstream and out of the swim, taking fish with it. This will be achieved by practice, where the angler will

Always watch a feeder as it swings back before the cast. The angler can then judge the precise moment to power the rod.

develop a 'feel' for just the right consistency, but I would advise compacting the feeder on the solid side – a little tug on the line will soon free the groundbait once on the bottom.

A smooth action is required when casting a groundbait-filled feeder, or the feed will soon be jerked out. With the rod held high in the vertical position, let the terminal rig swing behind, then with a smooth continuing movement, cast directly overhead at the target. In deep water – say, more than ten feet – a feeder must be allowed to fall freely once it has hit the water. To stop the line as the feeder enters the water, allowing it to fall to the bottom on a tight line, is counteractive to the basic idea of the method. If it is stopped at entry and left to fall on a tight line, the terminal rig will fall in an arc and end up well inside the line at which the loosened feed has settled, so spreading the feeding area unnecessarily. Once the feeder has settled, it is most important to lift the rod, straightening out the terminal tackle and preventing the feeder from lying across the line. Should any fish take the bait, there will be free movement of line through the bead or swivel.

Bite Detection

By far the most common form of bite indication used in bream fishing is the quiver tip. Both pleasure angler and matchman will have faith in their skills to pick out bites with a balanced tip, using either feeder or straight leger. A lined target board can be helpful, where the smallest fraction of tip movement can be detected, while in windy conditions a butt indicator is useful when the top half of the rod can be submerged.

The Swingtip

One of the most enjoyable methods of catching stillwater bream is to use a swingtip. The

Target board bite indicator. A small movement of the tip is easily picked out.

Pendulum bite indicator used for finicky bream.

tip hangs from the end of the rod by means of a small length of rubber tubing available in moulded form, having a pre-set angle for the angler to work from. I much prefer a piece of straight silicone rubber, where any preferred angle can be obtained by reeling in a little more line.

To cast with a swingtip rig is a little more difficult than with a standard quiver rod, in that the tip itself is prone to tangle. With care, however, a slow perpendicular cast will rarely tangle. The angler should allow the terminal rig to hang backwards, before casting high into the air, feathering the line as it approaches the desired spot. The leger is allowed to fall freely, after which the line is tightened until the tip points at the leger. Following a brief period, in which the line settles to its depth, the tip will drop once more, and is adjusted to the point where it hangs at an angle of around 45 degrees. When a bite is forthcoming, the tip will rise as a fish takes line, or fall when the weight of the leger is taken by the fish. In all cases, the strike is left until the movement is positive to ensure it is not a 'line bite'. I have always believed the swingtip to be the most delicate of all the bite indication methods, and, in my opinion, the most enjoyable.

The specimen bream angler, who usually fishes in darkness, will pin his faith in the bobbin and/or optonic set-up as described in Chapter 1. There are others, some simple and effective but many terribly over-complicated. All do but one job: they indicate to the angler that a fish has taken his bait.

Successful Hooking

I must confess to having what is virtually a fixation that the bite of a bream must be left to develop, more so in the early stages of a session. This is the period when bream settle on an area, when the angler may encounter what are known as 'line bites', where the tip jerks round periodically as bream rub against it. What is happening here is that the bream are moving into the swim, picking at tit-bits washed up in the water by their movement, and though difficult to ignore by a bream-crazy angler, they must, at all costs, be left alone; bream do not feed by jerking the tip round a foot at a time. A sensible approach is to wait for the tip to go round slowly. It may be an inch, where the fish has stopped to pick up more food, or it may be a few inches where, possibly, the bream has felt resistance and becomes wary. In all cases, no matter how much movement, wait until the tip goes round and *stays* round. This is the time to lift into the fish, though never to strike, for by this time the hook will be well into the mouth of the bream; all that is required is to put the point home. Generally speaking, the thing to do now is to hold the rod high: the bream will rise to the surface and can be brought gently to the net.

During my years of match fishing, a colleague named Les Sanders and I managed to keep a little thing to ourselves for a couple of seasons. For years we had thrown in thousands of balls of groundbait laced with casters, fishing bread or casters on the hook. One day, unable to raise a bite on anything whatsoever, I tried a paste made straight from my groundbait bowl – kneaded groundbait with a few crushed casters in it. Using a lump big enough to cover a size 6 hook, I caught over 100lb of Severn bream, none more than two pounds, in less than five hours, with Les enjoying a similar net. I still catch many bream with groundbait paste, though it is rare to see it used elsewhere.

Perhaps paradoxically, I have found that bream can go off a particular bait quite fast. An angler can be catching well, when for some inexplicable reason, the bream go off the feed and it seems they have deserted the swim. What in fact happens – and I am quite

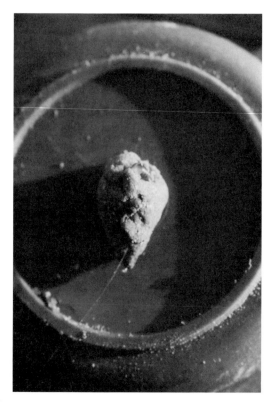

Paste made from groundbait and crushed casters. One of the deadliest bream hookbaits known to the author.

convinced of this – is that, unknown to the angler, he has at some time either pricked a fish, or maybe bashed it on the head with a falling feeder which spooked it and the rest of the shoal. Another reason could be that he has overfed them with one particular bait.

The thing to do now is to change hookbaits, and invariably the bream will once again start to feed. From the inertia of casters it may be wise to use a bait with movement, such as a worm/caster combination, or a couple of gozzers. A red-dyed maggot is in vogue during the writing of this book, which, when used with a caster as a cocktail, is a productive combination. The maggot is lightly hooked in the vent gristle first, followed by the caster, which will assist in preventing the maggot from curling over the point of the hook.

There are times when a change from the accepted bait is needed, when the angler needs to do something entirely different. Many years ago, Cofton were due to compete in a team match on the Warwickshire Avon. Though team matches are approached with a defensive attitude, with section points more important than personal glory, we felt that bream could play a big part in the forthcoming event. The contest was to be held at Eckington, a deeper area of the river where big bream shoals lived, bream which were notoriously hard to catch in summer, never mind winter! The river, low and clear with frost, with not a breath of wind to ripple the surface, looked anything but breamy. I will not dwell too much on the build-up, suffice to say that after spending four hours on redworms/gozzers/casters, I put on a size 6 hook, and squeezed on a large piece of caster-flavoured groundbait paste. Five big Avon bream came to the net, all of which rewrote the book, virtually pulling the rod off the rest. As I have said before, there are no hard and fast rules in fishing, only guides.

There is no doubt that the feeder approach is effective at most times, but there are also occasions when more subtle tactics will pay dividends. In 1976, Cofton won the *Angling Times* Winter League, the final being held at Coombe Abbey Lake, near Coventry. We knew the method would be to fish for bream with a long-range quiver-tip rig, but as the event was to take place at the very beginning of the season we had no time for practice. Thankfully, the organization was first class.

The whole squad attended practice sessions held at Patshull Park, near Wolverhampton, a large complex housing a number of trout pools. There, on the seclusion of an unused trout lake, and with kind permission of the manager, we catapulted groundbait for hours

on end at a marker buoy anchored out at fifty yards. When everyone could all but hit the marker buoy every time, we changed to our own personal choice of quiver-tip rod with a ¾oz bomb, tied to a 2.6lb reel line. After a while we could all place the bomb alongside the buoy at each cast; on the day penultimate to the match, we knew we were ready. The annals of match angling record that Cofton won the contest with pounds to spare, a direct result of homework, practice and species knowledge. (As Coombe is a relatively shallow lake, the groundbait, laced with casters, had to be of a sloppy nature, which broke up immediately on hitting the surface, so dropping to the bream in a natural manner. Any suggestions of a hard lump crashing in sent the bream scattering in all directions. I often wonder if a feeder in those days would have resulted in a similar exodus – and to take the matter further – does it do so today?)

Straight Legering

There is a lot to be said for the standard quiver-tip in preference to the feeder. The matter of finesse can be taken to whatever lengths may be necessary, on those hard winter days when a 1lb hooklength is called for, or when the bite is no more than a minuscule pull. On days such as these, the feeder, no matter how well balanced, can be an encumbrance. Other occasions, when a straight lead set-up may be desired are when fishing at extreme distance or excessive depths.

The aerodynamic precision of the Arlesey bomb is ideal for legering at distance, and should be at least ¾oz in weight, heavier if the distance is extreme. With my dislike for hardware, I stretch a piece of stretchable boom line from a Drennan Link-Leger to about 8in, and cut off the threaded nylon end. This leaves a leger-link complete with the hole for threading to the reel line, on to which the bomb is tied using a tucked half-blood knot. To commence, a 4ft hooklength of 1.7–2.6lb b/s is about right; this can be lengthened if bites are not forthcoming, or if they are just finicky touches, failing to develop into a full take. At times I have lengthened this tail to more than 6ft before the bream have taken with confidence, and while this may seem long, the fact remains that it was necessary – anything shorter and the fish simply dropped the bait time after time.

The fear of terminal rigs becoming tangled is always uppermost in the mind. I have seen some weird ideas on how to keep the hooklength in a semi-floating situation, from bits of cork glued to the line to tiny balls of polystyrene threaded on. All of these methods do the job quite well, but perhaps there is no need for any of this. Once the terminal tackle has settled on the bottom, it can be lifted gently to straighten out the hooklength, and you can be assured that when lift-

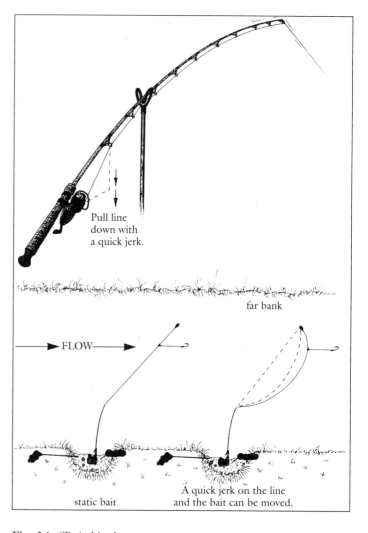

Fig. 16 'Twitching'.

ed, the weight of the leger – or feeder – will take it to the bottom fast, leaving the hooklength to settle gently. In this manner it will foul nothing.

The art of twitching the hookbait when breaming cannot be overemphasized. Time and time again I have remained biteless, though when I commenced to twitch the bait along the bottom I have taken fish after fish. I look at it as the 'cat and mouse syndrome':

where the cat looks at the mouse for minutes on end, and when the poor old mouse makes a move it's curtains. Could it be that fish have the same teasing nature?

The initial cast is made to the far side of the baited area, to either right or left. If, after a sensible time, no bites are forthcoming, the twitching pattern is commenced by pulling the bait towards the bank a couple of inches

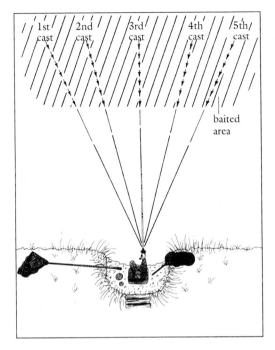

Fig. 17 Twitching pattern for stillwaters.

at a time, until it is considered the bait is out of the area. The next cast should be a foot or so towards the centre of the area, and the pattern continued until the whole of the baited area has been covered. It will be noticed that many bites come immediately after the bait has been moved, and sometimes as it is moving. In these cases the bite indication is positive, for any bream mouthing the bait will feel the weight of the pull, and nine times out of ten will have the bait well into its mouth. The fish rises to the horizontal and bolts, therefore hooking itself.

RIVER BREAM

It does not take a genius to realize that by virtue of their flat shape, river bream will not adapt readily to fast waters. They tend to live in deeper, more placid areas, more often than not in large shoals, with each shoal containing fish of all sizes as in a family situation.

For an angler visiting a strange venue, it can be quite daunting to choose where to fish for bream, but it's not too difficult to find them. Most rivers I know which are of a deep, even nature are the home of bream, yet rivers which look to be of an even bottom usually have depths which alter quite dramatically, where a level ten feet drops to fifteen feet before rising to the normal depth once again. It is in such places that you will find bream, for any depression in the river bed is a natural spot for food to be gathered, washed down by the current. These holes, some extremely large, will have little or no current whatsoever, for the stream will pass over the top, and they are a natural place for bream to congregate. Even faster stretches of the middle Severn have deep holes and you can bet your last penny bream live there. The inside of a wide bend in the river, usually much slower than the outside, is another natural holding place for bream. Another breamy spot is where the river widens before reverting to its original width, a place where the current noticeably slows down.

The basic principles explained in the stillwater section apply in similar fashion to river bream, but tackle needs that little extra strength to counteract current, though nothing extreme where the balance suffers. A quiver-tip rod capable of casting a medium open-end feeder thirty to forty yards is advisable, preferably a ten-foot rod with a medium tip. (Note the word 'medium': river bream fishing requires nothing too sloppy, too stiff, too weak or too strong.) Reel line should be of 3.2lb b/s, enough to cast a full feeder, yet thin enough to counteract a good current. It may be felt that a stronger line would be a further insurance, but the problem then arises that the thicker, stronger line would create a greater line area for the current to push against, which means more lead has to be used, which in turn means a stronger rod, and so on In extreme cases, where an exceptionally long-distance cast is required, a shock leader of 4.4lb can be tied into the reel line. This shock leader is used to take the initial strain of a strong cast, but once out of the rod rings does nothing to impair the distance. Five yards is an adequate length for this, using full blood knots to keep a low profile.

Any medium open-end feeder will suffice, as long as it has the facility to add or remove lead when necessary, using the terminal arrangement explained earlier. Other terminal rigs may incorporate two swivels, one for the feeder-link and one for the hooklength, for use in a faster current where hookbait and feeder could possibly spin, causing tangles. When using a swivel, a good idea is to cover it with silicone tubing to prevent line fouling.

On a river with a steady flow, say around two knots per hour, there will be no need to use extra lead as the feeder will carry enough in its original state. Should the current pick up at any time, just add enough lead to enable the feeder to hold bottom.

The straight legering method is very productive in times of coloured water, and river bream react very favourably to such conditions as long as the water temperature is stable or, better still, rising. Without the weight of the feeder to consider, lighter lines can be used with all factors balanced to each other. Small redworms or maggots are by far the best baits, though any groundbaiting should be very sparse after the initial introduction. A longer than normal hooklength is advisable, with six feet quite acceptable. As with most

fish in coloured water, the bite of a bream is positive; the tip goes round in a continuous movement, though when taking advantage of lighter lines care must be taken to lift slowly but solidly into the fish.

On the other hand, when fishing in exceptionally clear conditions, fish can see any line you may use no matter how thin, and detect any unnatural action in the hookbait. In such adverse conditions, straight legering is the only way to present tackle so fine it may seem unbalanced. I remember one hot, sunny day on the Huntspill when the only way I could raise a bite was by using ¾lb hooklengths of six feet in length, using a size 22 hook. As the day wore on, I experimented with stronger line until by dusk I was catching fish using 2.6lb direct to a size 10 hook.

In slower, shallower rivers, another variation is to present the bait in a manner where bream take the bait 'on the drop' as it falls through the water. If it is felt that bream are off the bottom, feeding at mid-water, the hooklength can be lengthened to around eight feet; any more than this and difficulty will be experienced when casting. This form of fishing requires a leger of just enough weight to cast, and the rod must be held whenever possible for the take can occur at just about any time, from surface to bottom. Loose feed is preferable to groundbait, introduced on the little and often principle to keep the shoal interested. A bite is usually a straightening out of the tip as a fish takes the weight of the lead; the resulting strike should be longer than normal to take out the slack line.

So much for bream. They are a pleasant fish to catch, not too difficult to predict, but at the same time can drive an angler crackers.

9   Chub

Should an angler cast his baited hook in the vicinity of a wise old chub, and should that chub be hungry, and should the bait be free from nauseating aromas such as nicotine, after-shave or petrol, etc. and also free of any encumbrance which makes it perform differently from loose offerings, and if the chub has not seen the angler, or sensed heavy footfalls, then – with luck – the chub might just be conned enough to taste the hookbait. Most times it will not.

The chub inhabits almost all of the rivers and streams of England and Wales, though is perhaps rare in Scotland, and completely unknown in Ireland. This is their sad loss, for the species is a fine fighter, growing to weights approaching 10lb.

BAITS

Chub are a fish that enjoy a varied diet, and are blessed with a mouth so large that a 6lb fish could hide a tennis ball without it touching the sides. They scoff maggots and casters by the million. They rise to hatching nymphs and egg-laying duns, crashing to the surface in the urgency, while another day will see the same chub sip delicately at a piece of floating crust. A lump of cubed luncheon meat measuring one inch in all directions will be swallowed in an instant by even a half-pound chub. They will eat virtually anything which

is edible and which can be taken in their mouths, including other fish, frogs, crayfish and elvers.

The liking chub have for fruit is unusual: a piece of apple or pear is readily chomped at, as is banana, but above all, there is one fruit that shoal-size chub take with gusto. If the angler has access to a weirpool on any chub-holding river, all he then needs is a ten-foot medium-action leger rod, a few ball legers, a packet of size 6 eyed hooks, a reel loaded with 4.4lb line – and a couple of pounds of cherries. The method is simplicity in itself. The stone need not be removed, for the hook is stuck in the fleshy part of the cherry, but I prefer to dig the stone out, letting the juices flow freely. The method is to cast the terminal rig upstream, allowing it to bounce round on the bottom, controlling the line just enough to keep in touch with the leger. When a chub takes this bait there is no warning – just a wallop of the rod end as it curves into a hooked fish. Loose feeding is not really necessary, but if the angler feels that he simply must throw in hookbait samples, then he must tread very carefully; if the cherries are not eaten immediately, the fish will chase the smell downstream and out of the swim. Chubbing with cherries is a short-lived season, but used in the warm-water months of summer can result in a most satisfying day out.

Another excellent chub bait is a big, black slimy slug. Whereas we have a wormery to store worms, there is no such tender treatment for slugs; they must be collected and used fairly quickly. I do not intend to suggest places where slugs can be found, for while the crayfish is disappearing slugs thrive by the million and they can be found anywhere there is vegetation. Many specialist anglers feel the slug is a bait for summer chub only, but I have used them quite successfully in all seasons as long as they are around garden and meadow, though to search during early morning is essential, for as the daylight increases, so do slugs disappear.

The crayfish – our freshwater 'lobster' – must now be in danger of becoming extinct, for the clear Worcestershire streams where I once hunted crayfish are now virtually devoid of them. But how the chub loves to crunch them down. Should the reader be fortunate in having access to streams where crayfish continue to thrive, he could do worse than to anchor a small net of fine mesh on the bottom, baited with bits of meat or other forms of food. After half an hour or so, the net must be retrieved; any crayfish found hanging in the netting should be removed and plopped into a bucket of water. Most streams of this nature are shallow, and to wade upstream, lifting stones under which crayfish hide is much more fun, though care must be taken; the nip from the leading pincers of a crayfish, though not too painful, is enough to make the crayfisher drop his prize. To work upstream is a necessity, as the moving of the stones releases mud and silt, which clouds the water to an impenetrable murk.

Perhaps above all other baits, breadcrust is the bait chub prefer. There is some indefinable magic in casting a piece of crust near the roots of a willow, or under the shadow of a raft. Using the lightest of legers, in some cases no more than one swan shot, the cast is made upstream of where the bites may be expected, where the bait will settle slowly into the easy water where chub lie. Loose line must be gathered in the free hand, as flyfishers do, unless the angler prefers to reel in any slack. The bite, more often than not, is picked out by the line becoming sloppy as a fish picks up the bait. When the bait is downstream, a good pull will be a more likely indication.

The piece of crust is torn from a loaf which is not too fresh; one about two days old is ideal as the crust will be a bit tougher, making it stay on the hook longer. The tail for fishing the crust needs to be longer than for most baits, for the semi-buoyancy of a piece of crust allows it to wave in the current. Two feet is not overlong, and if it is suspected that the chub are going to be finicky, four feet is a safer bet. Bread in flake form is equally effective, and in certain conditions, such as water which is less than clear, flake gives an added bonus when the tiny morsels which break away act as a fine attractor. Fish sample these morsels, which assist in overcoming their natural caution.

Cheese has long been associated with chub, an aromatic bait which accounts for many big fish each season. Any of the cheeses will suffice, but the varieties which carry the most pungent smells are much the better choice. It should be fresh, for cheese which has been left in the open for any length of time loses its flavour. As a bait which is composed of fats, cheese solidifies in colder water and needs to be presented in paste form to retain its softness, but without losing the enticing smells. Cornflour is a great softener of cheese as it will not add any unwanted flavours. The cheese should be grated into a bowl, and the cornflour added a little at a time, kneaded in a clean cloth until the paste becomes soft, yet remaining solid enough to stay on the hook. It can be seen just how attractive paste must be to fish when a lump is left in a bowl of clear water. The immediate surrounding area becomes clouded as the surface of the paste washes out, with an aroma which will entice chub from a long way downstream.

With legering techniques specifically, chub are a species that do not respond to cereal groundbait. When I have used it in a feeder, it's usual to take a couple of chub at the most before they disappear. It may be they follow the groundbait particles downstream, but a more logical explanation would be that they find cloud bait not to their liking – they are much too greedy to be satisfied by it.

Meat in its various forms – luncheon, sausage, bacon grill, raw steak, etc. – are also baits which take toll of chub of all sizes, at all times. The method is covered in detail in Chapter 5.

HABITAT

Chub, roach, bream, barbel and every other species have their favourite areas, be it gravel beds, slower or faster water, and, depending on times of the season, favourite places to move to. This, however, comes only with experience. In his early days, the angler must watch and enquire, and once again I must stress that the local tackle shop is always a good source of information.

Small chub, those under two pounds, can be found just about anywhere, from shallows to deeps, in all seasons. They are a shoal fish, with a strong sense of social structure where fish of a size tend to swim together. Big chub, in a manner similar to barbel, are almost loners, but it is noticeable that if a sizeable chub

sandstone

roach

chub

barbel

Fig. 18 Typical section of undercut bank on an outside bend of the river Teme.

is hooked and landed safely, there will be a fish of a similar size in the swim willing to take the bait. This pairing of chub is a pattern I have found true to form over years of fishing, and though I have yet to determine the possibility of one male and one female 'living' together, it would make sweet romantic reading should this be so.

On rivers blessed with covered banks, such as the Teme, Severn and Wye, chub will be found in the edges, dwelling among tree roots, always close to cover. They prefer to live under a ceiling, be it the leafy branches of alder or willow, or where a raft has formed by a stretching bough of a tree catching debris floating downstream. Other natural haunts are holes cut into the bank by currents, such as on a small river on the outside of a bend, or at the top end of an island. In the low, clear water of summer, chub play hide and seek under the masses of thick streamer weed which grow prodigiously on these rivers. The side and tail end of weirpools along any river are always a good bet, while the areas below inlet streams are worth a few hours' fishing, as are those parts of a river which shelve up from a deep hole into moving water.

A weir pool of the Hertfordshire Lugg. The slack on the far side is full of good chub and pike.

On flat, almost featureless rivers such as the redirected waterways of the Broads, the Ouse around Newport Pagnell, or the middle and tidal Trent, the finding of chub is more difficult. The angler is faced with mile upon mile of river with nothing to determine where he should fish, yet it is these rivers which are home to great numbers of chub, growing to quite sizeable proportions. Therefore, the miles of barren treeless banks of some rivers leave the angler – and perhaps the chub – with problems. In these situations, eye and ear are the best detectors. The weekly river reports always carry stories of who caught what, where and how they fished, and it becomes apparent that certain areas of a river always produce chub, whereas other areas do not.

FEEDERLESS CHUBBING

Straight legering, where the angler watches his tip for bite indication, or touch legering where he feels the line for a biting fish, are exciting ways of catching chub, especially the big ones. There can be no doubt that specimen-size fish fall more easily to a straight leger approach, for as big chub frequent snaggy haunts, the encumbrance of any surplus tackle such as a feeder is noisy, bulky and all too unnecessary. If this method is employed, the angler should be very aware that chub are a fish that rise to a bait. If a constant supply of maggot or casters are poured into a river containing chub, sooner or later they will appear, taking the bait inches under the surface, moving with a speed which can smash a hook-

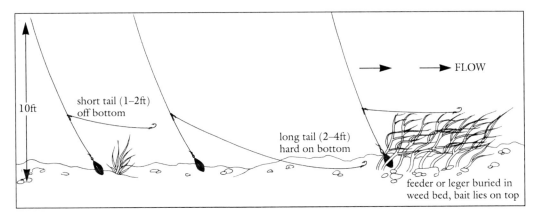

Fig. 19 Bait actions in flowing water.

length in a blink. The leger angler, who needs to shoal his fish on the bottom, must therefore be very careful with loose feed, or his chub will soon come up in the water. He can, however, capitalize on this greedy chub behaviour by putting the larder of food on the bed of the river. On a swim with good depth – say eight feet or more – a bait dropper is an excellent device with which to put loose feed directly on the bottom.

As chub prefer to live near snags or other avenues of escape, in any form of legering where snags are prevalent, it is sensible to use a lead or feeder-link of a much weaker breaking strain than that of the reel line. Should the lead or feeder snag up, this will be the only loss, breaking off at a sensible time, whereas to strain on rod and line for minutes on end can seriously damage the angler's nerve, his tackle and his swim.

In an ideal situation, with balanced tackle and without a root or sunken branch to worry about, a reel line of 2.6lb to a hooklength of 1.7lb would catch any chub which swims; it would simply be a matter of time. However, depending on known snags or more visible means of line breakage, this line needs to be stepped up more than the angler may at first

believe. Following a bite which may be most tentative, the first dash of a big, well-hooked chub will test rod, line and angler to their limits. Whereas a barbel will head upstream and out, the chub dives inside, looking for those roots or other snags in which to escape. Once in a mass of roots or whatever – especially if a feeder is used – the angler can usually say good-bye to his fish as there is very little that can be done. When straight legering, the old ploy of putting down the rod, leaving line to run freely off the reel, can sometimes be effective, but more often than not will result in the fish pulling more line into the snag. Far better I think is to heave mightily on the rod as the chub runs, trying to prevent him reaching the snags. At times this will be effective, while at other times the hook may pull out or the line may break – a sad ending, but perhaps not the dramatic underwater scene one may believe: a chub or any other fish can get rid of a hook in minutes, especially if it is of the barbless pattern. Line, therefore, should be increased in strength if any snags are in the vicinity. Obviously, this may result in fewer bites, but the fish that take the bait will at least be landed.

With small, shoal chub as the target, the size of hook must be based on the hookbait

Even a size 10 hook can be lost in a 3lb Chub.

the actual shape of a flattened crystal hook, it becomes clear that once the point is home to the bend, the constant pressure from the rod keeps it in there. Unless the hook breaks, the only way it can be removed is by pulling backwards, quite irrespective of what it is hooked into!

FEEDERING FOR CHUB

Visit any hard-fished venue where chub are predominant, and anglers everywhere will be seen heaving mightily to cast a feeder close to the far bank. Though this may seem unnecessary – and sometimes it is – a feeder constantly well placed at distance can attract chub from far downstream. This will leave the near bank swim to be used for another method – be it float or a light link-leger – which makes the ploy of the long-distance feeder technique a sound idea.

Moreover, a bite from a fish at long distance is easier to make safe contact with. This may be difficult for the inexperienced to understand, but anglers who have caught fish of any size will talk about 'cracking off', where the hooklength breaks on a strike. At distance, this is alleviated to some extent, for the stretch factor of the extra line has a cushioning effect on the instant strain put into a line upon a hard strike; the shorter the distance, the more chance it will have of cracking off. This is another situation where a bow of line is let from the reel once the feeder has settled, and a bite is registered by the bow tightening up, or becoming larger as a fish moves the feeder, or by small bounces of the rod tip as a chub mouths the bait. These long-distance bites do not need a hard strike; it is more of a fast lift, after which the weight of feeder and water pressure on the line will set the hook.

used. Should it be maggot or caster, a hook of size 14 to 20 would be adequate, preferably of the flattened crystal-bend type, of which a Kamasan B920 pattern would be an excellent choice.

There is no doubt that even small chub can be quite hook shy, refusing to accept any bait which is not compatible in behaviour with the loose feed. For instance, a maggot which attempts to pull a size 12 hook along the bottom will behave very differently from a brother maggot moving almost normally with a size 20 hook stuck in its posterior. It never ceases to amaze me that a hook of such tiny proportions will successfully land fish of quite a large size, but when one stops to consider

The tackle requirements, baits and methods are similar to those of barbel, though with everything scaled down. The rod should be of the medium-action quiver-tip type, where a medium or small blockend can be cast with accuracy into the aforementioned places, entering the water with as little disturbance as possible. Reel line need be no more than 3.2lb, with a hooklength of 2.6lb.

The initial feeding pattern requires a fair amount of feed to be put down, where the medium blockend is used attached to a short tail with a small swivel. Though chub do eat hempseed, any great amounts as used in barbel fishing will sicken them, so it is much better to leave it out altogether; maggots or casters are quite adequate for feedering, and will catch shoal chub in quantity. Once the angler considers that enough feed has been introduced, he must scale down the feeder to a slimline version, using the minimum amount of weight needed to hold bottom.

Winter heralds bingo time for the specialist chub angler and he, of all people, will know that to put too much feed into a swim is to ask for trouble. It is a time to put in the minimum of loose feed, when even a small feeder-full will be too much.

SMALL STREAM CHUB

Fishing for chub on a clear stream in summer must be one of the most enjoyable types of fishing. To walk green meadows, stopping at chubby-looking spots, and to rest against tall willows is so soul-consuming that a full day will pass all too quickly. Should the angler know his river he can visit old haunts, angling for fish he may have taken prisoner on a previous day. Should he, however, be visiting an unknown river, he would do well to walk the banks, marking prospective spots before mounting his attack.

In daytime, chub will be hidden amongst streamer weed, or under rafts, perhaps in a deep hole near the bank. Wherever they may be, the slightest sign of threat will send them shooting off to safety, into undercut banks, deep weed and the like. The approach should be quiet, with the angler keeping low, or taking advantage of a bush or tree to eliminate his profile against the sky. A few minutes with a pair of polaroid glasses are well worth spending, and it is surprising just how many fish will be seen once the angler's eyes have adjusted.

Within walking distance of my home is the tiny River Salwarpe. One of my favourite pastimes is to hide in the growth of the steep banks along the lower reaches, flicking in bits of bread. If I choose my spot well and find a swim with shadow, I see the occasional white blob appear under the water as a big chub opens its mouth to take in food. If it is high in the water, a huge bulge pushes up the water as the chub turns down. One bump, however, one careless footfall and it would

A deep glide between shallows. An ideal spot for chub.

seem there is not one chub in the river. As an experiment, to witness first hand just how wary chub are, find a shoal of small fish that you can see, and stamp lightly on the bank. I can guarantee that you will not see one chub left in that swim.

The wise chub angler travels lightly: a rod, reel and landing-net are all he requires, with a tackle bag slung across his shoulders to carry essential items such as legers, bait and refreshments. There is no place here for the gentle quivertip rod, nor for the lumpy feeder type, for this is traditional specimen hunting at its finest, where a two-piece medium-action cane rod cannot be bettered. Reel line should be no less than 5lb, which is perhaps strong by the standards of some, but when I recall the happy days spent on my

Steve Lees chub fishing under the far bank on the small Warwickshire Arrow.

home River Teme, a river with lush growth along its banks where trees grow into the water's edge, then 5lb line direct to the hook is just about adequate.

Nor is this a time for tiny baits such as maggot or casters. A loaf of crusty bread, some crayfish if wished, perhaps a portion of luncheon meat is all that the angler will need, while slug or worm can be collected at will. Another natural bait rarely used is the white grub, found under cow-pats. Despite consulting my library I can find no reference to this grub, but chub certainly do love them. One on a size 10 hook is ample, and as long as the angler is quiet in his approach he will soon find out if a chub is in the vicinity.

Crayfish are hooked in the fleshy part of the second body segment, using a hook

Fishing to a 'character' within a swim. Chub lie in the shadow of mid-river reeds.

balanced to the size of the bait. A good-sized cray of 1–2in will take a size 6 hook with ease, and with a hook of this size it's perhaps wise to use an eyed variety in preference to the spade end. A Drennan Starpoint is an excellent choice, an eyed hook with a unique direct strike design. A fighting mad chub changes direction many times, and there is always the possibility that as the line rubs against the spade, taking the strain from directly up the hook shank to a sideways position, the spade – which can be quite sharp – may cut the line where it rubs against the edge.

In general terms, big chub much prefer big baits, and if this is borne in mind the angler can be selective and discount smaller nuisance fish. While most of the natural baits can be freelined in shallow swims, the rolling leger technique will give the angler some control over his terminal tackle in deeper areas, thus enabling him to lessen the amount of bow in the line created by the current. When the angler feels his bait has reached a chubby-looking haunt he can hold the line, feeling for the bite. This can vary, from a slackening of the line, to occasions when the chub loses all caution. When this occurs, and you, the angler, are not prepared, a running chub can take the rod out of your hands.

WINTER CHUBBING

The early part of winter, that first good flush which sends rivers a dirty shade of brown can be a nightmare to the angler. Debris which for months has been lying on the bank gets washed away – plastic bottles, food containers of all descriptions,

autumn leaves by the million, banks of weed, trees, drowned animals and anything else which is not fixed. I will never forget the occasion on the Severn, when, following the January rains of 1990, a newly painted green and white shed floated by, complete with veranda, steps, two potted geraniums and a shiny brass padlock.

To a good leger angler, however, winter can also be a season to take advantage of. Match anglers up and down the country, in the never-ending quest to fill their shelves with trophies, have developed methods particular to their home rivers. The Severn angler will catch on legered meat, the chub of Yorkshire go bonkers for wasp grub, while the suspicious chub of the Trent, ignoring the former delicacies, eat lobworms with gusto. Strangely, to use a home method on another river is probably to remain fishless – yet another fishy mystery which I cannot understand.

The method of legered (unfrozen) wasp grub is fairly straightforward, where a feeder can be used, filled with crushed wasp cake, with one or two grubs to a size 14 hook, or a

Though more like the 'Everglades' of America, this is a flooded River Severn at Worcester.

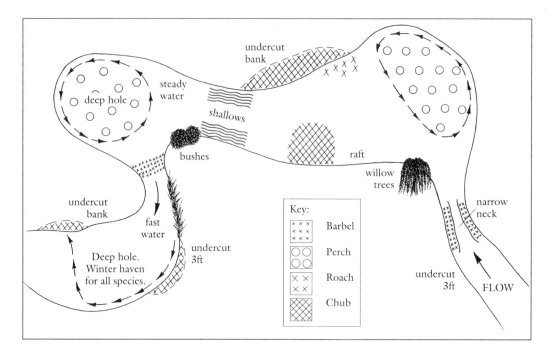

Fig. 20 Small river location.

small piece of the cake on a size 10. When using wasp cake or grubs as bait, there is no need to fish with too fine a hooklength, for should a chub decide it wants to eat this bait, it would still do so if it was tied to a length of clothes line. (For those days when the angler senses that only one or two bites will be forthcoming, a straight leger may be more productive, cast down the margins into slower water.) Hook size, too, is of little relevance when using a large piece of cake, as an eyed size 4 does not look at all out of place when stuck in the mouth of even a 1lb chub. I would suggest, however, that the barb of a hook of this size needs to be broken off or filed down, or the penetration of the hook may be hindered. The mouth of a chub is solid muscle.

The legered lobworm technique of the Trent is no doubt applicable to rivers elsewhere, though after many attempts to catch a Severn chub on a worm, I have yet to be successful. The rod for fishing the lob needs to be quite strong for fishing a swim out in the current, where a ten-foot stiff-action feeder rod would not go amiss, using line of around 5lb direct to a size 10 or even an 8 hook. This is no time for balanced legers. Trent anglers have, in fact, developed what they call a 'lobby-lead': a flattened lump of lead, home moulded, which sits on the bottom of a rushing river as would a half-housebrick. Excellent as these leads may be, a coffin lead or flattened Arlesey bomb will suffice, heavy enough to sit hard on the bottom.

Bites on lobworm can vary from a series of hard tugs to the rod forming a U-bend as the fish hooks itself. The latter is difficult to miss, but the tugs must be ignored, which is quite hard for a fishless angler. I believe – and it is once more only an educated guess – that these

The Severn at Holt Fleet. Almost 'normal' winter level.

tugs are the result of chub who want the worm so badly that they try to free it from whatever is holding it, in this case the hook. Whatever the true reason may be, this is one time when fish abandon their strong sense of self-preservation, when a bait so unnatural in behaviour is chomped at with vigour. In the matchfishing context, the anchoring of the worm is necessary to keep the bait with the allotted swim, but in a more natural environment, this is detrimental to the catching of fish. Worms if necessary washed into the river rarely settle in one spot as they are carried by the current, rising and falling, moving along the bed at whatever speed the current dictates. Chub take these worms on the move, and they don't mess around when they take them; should they stop to ponder, another hungry competitor will soon chomp the worm away.

There can be no doubt that the 'back-end' of winter – the last two months of the season – is the time when big chub are caught in greater numbers than the rest of the season put together. Following the high water of winter floods, rivers become clean once again, flowing with warmer water, preparing to harbour new life. The months following this period is the time when fish prepare to spawn, when they stock up energy, taking more food than normal.

Holt bridge at summer level.

Yet again, big chub continue to be choosy. But when the chub man is successful in hooking his fish, the somewhat lethargic fight of the summer chub is replaced by the hard, plunging, sheer doggedness of the winter fish. It could be a different species.

I am a great believer that big fish are most careful in selecting food. A chub over 5lb must be the most finicky of fish, and to persuade it to take hooked bait is, at times, impossible. As a chub grows older he doesn't chase around. He prefers to eat as much food as he needs in the shortest time possible, where one big mouthful is looked for in preference to minute morsels. Gone are the days when as a daft, suicidal shoal fish, the chub chased around at handfuls of maggots or casters, spending more time in a keepnet than out of it. Older, and after suffering the indignity of the hook many times, his life is placid as he waits for hunger, and food, to approach. Would that big old chub join his greedy offspring chasing loose feed, or would he meander safely around, looking for slug, crayfish or lobworm?

10　Roach

The roach, above all other fish, gives me – and I suspect most other anglers – the greatest of piscatorial pleasure. The ease in catching them (small ones anyway), the delight of their colour, the gentle manner in feeding habits, all go together to complete the pinnacle of angling enjoyment.

My earliest recollections of roach are those I caught from the Warwickshire Arrow outside the tiny hamlet of Broome. This sleepy part of the river lies no more than one mile from the confluence with the Shakespearian Avon, itself a very good roach river. Just upstream from the road bridge is an old mill, the remains still visible today, though it is not in use. Below the race of the millstream, the river widens a little, slowing considerably as it flows under the bridge, after which the banks become edged with willows, and it was here, with my old two-piece bamboo rod and a line of sewing cotton, that I caught many wondrous roach, crimson-finned and black-backed, small-river roach that fought with honour. My favourite bait then was the same as it always has been – a piece of simple breadflake squeezed on to a size 14 hook – the bait which has accounted for the vast majority of my biggest roach.

BAITS

Maggots will catch more fish than any other bait, and roach are no exception. Used in ones or twos, the maggot will take fish after fish as long as the little and often principle is observed when loose feeding. A small hook is necessary, no more than a size 20 for a single bait, with perhaps an 18 for doubles. I much prefer a link-leger for roaching down the nearside edge of a river, is where a small Drennan Feeder-Link is unbeatable, for it can hold less than a dozen maggots, keeping the feed down to minimum. Any balance of lead can be adjusted by adding or subtracting swan shot to the piece of line sticking out of the bottom.

Casters will always produce slightly bigger fish, but care must be taken in mounting them. A size 18 hook can be buried with ease inside a caster, making the presentation so much better, and though you may think the hooking properties are affected, you will find a fish will be well hooked, whereas a caster just nicked on a hook can result in missed bites. Hempseed and casters go well together; but once again, it is all too easy to overfeed.

Legered tares are a good summer bait, and used in conjunction with hempseed can be a killing method, but, above all, the angler must sit with the rod in his hand. He will have but one shot at a bite, and if this is missed you can bet your last maggot the bait will be gone. When using tares there is no need to go too fine on line strengths. Reel line of 2.6lb will be adequate, with a hook-length of 1.7lb; a size 14 hook is certainly

A good net of roach caught on legered tares. The barbel was a 'nice surprise'.

not too big for a single tare, which although looking a bit daft will be accepted quite willingly by roach. If the chosen swim is too far into the river to be fed by hand, a small Drennan Feeder-Link full of hempseed will be ideal, attached without stretching the link, giving a 2in length.

Let me now stick my head on the block and dispense with a long-standing tradition. In my experience, the much beloved tail of a lobworm for winter roaching is just about useless. First of all, the worm dies pretty quickly, so losing the all-important movement. Secondly, I cannot see any sense in using half of anything when a whole item of smaller size is available. A redworm is a much better roach bait in the coloured waters of winter and, mounted on a size 16 hook, has put many a fine roach into my net. This worm lives longer than any other variety when underwater, and is simply hooked once through the middle and left to wriggle enticingly; to stick the hook in more than one position would be to reduce the movement, also making the bait appear unnatural. The method of passing the

hook through more than once will give rise to the point of the hook being masked.

Breadflake is my favourite bait for specimen roach. I am no great believer in too much groundbait when roach fishing, but breadflake demands that just a little be used. The method of making groundbait as explained in Chapter 8 is unbeatable.

Roach have a quaint habit of rising in the water when feeding. Should bites develop and then cease for no apparent reason, it's a good idea to lengthen the hooklength, when it's possible to get bites 'on the drop' as the hookbait is falling. Strangely, the bite is more positive than when the bait is on the bottom, and a good legerman can increase his catch enormously in remembering this.

RIVER ROACH

If an angler is to be successful at catching roach, there are certain factors to consider. Though dreams of a fisherman may be filled with pictures of clear chuckling streams, and days of warm sunshine, the expert roach angler will groan at such conditions. The fact is that roach do not feed well in bright light. As the sun drops, however, and the shadows lengthen, roach gain confidence, feeding better as darkness approaches. Furthermore, take that same swim when the river is coloured with rain water and the story will be different yet again, when roach can go barmy from dawn to dusk. No fish responds better to coloured water than the roach and if the angler can judge his day, with perhaps a gentle breeze to ruffle the surface, then he will have all the chances in the world on his side.

For whatever reason, in the summer months at least, river roach prefer to live over a bed of gravel – perhaps they like to scratch their bellies. To locate these gravel beds is sometimes difficult, but if the angler wishes to catch big roach then he must be prepared to work a little. A sensitive leger rod, coupled with a 2oz bomb is ideal as a gravel detector. The angler must look for what he *thinks* is a good roach area, then walk along the bank, casting the bomb to various spots. Allow the bomb to scrape the bottom on retrieve; gravel beds are easily detected when the bomb grates and bumps along the stones.

As autumn approaches, roach come close to the bank, looking for easier water. Though they lie in the slack current of the margins, I have always found the crease between the main current and the slack to be the area where I can catch most fish. This, I believe, is the classic case of fish darting into the current to eat any passing food and then swimming back to the shoal. It may be thought that to fish the slack in the first place is the obvious thing to do, but the crease is where most fish will be found. It is vitally important to realize that nothing puts roach off quicker than overfeeding. It may be said that introducing twenty maggots every four minutes is similar to putting in five every minute, yet it is a fact that roach will respond favourably to a constant trickle, one big handful sends them well away from the swim. The suggestion which follows is beyond the patience of most anglers, but I have put this into practice with great success. If a swim is gently baited for a lengthy period – say up to an hour – introducing just a couple of maggots or casters at regular intervals of around thirty seconds, and without the angler putting in float, feeder or leger, any resident shoal of roach will settle down to a confident feeding pattern. To get

them to do this while running a float at them, or chucking in feeder or lead makes the whole thing much more difficult. Casting should therefore be kept to a minimum. When they commence feeding proper, bites can come quick and fast, but only if the shoal has been allowed to settle quietly.

There can be no doubt also that roach demand the ultimate in bait presentation. Throughout my match years, at top roach venues such as Stourport-on-Severn, Evesham, and parts of the Trent, roach to more than 2lb were regularly caught in matches. This was in the days of glass rods, yet 12oz hooklengths were commonplace. It was necessary to use such fine tackle on these hard-fished venues, for to present big roach with line much thicker was to fail miserably.

A welcome roach to a winter angler.

I have stated my belief that barbel prefer a still bait, and in like manner I believe roach prefer a bait which moves – but only just. The smallest of legers or swan-shot arrangements gives the angler the chance to move the bait fractionally as he wishes: just a tiny pull now and again, or a gentle lift of the rod which allows the leger to move downstream a fraction. The hooklength should be longer than normal, 4ft is certainly not too much, with everything else balanced to size of bait and speed of current.

Terminal tackle for roach must be carefully balanced. If the chosen swim is an inside slow swim, a wand could be ideal. Failing this, where a slightly stronger rig is needed, a light ten-foot tip-action rod is fine. I must stress yet again my dislike for beads, swivels or any other unnecessary encumbrance; this is roach fishing, where delicacy is the name of the game. A Drennan Leger-Link, or a lead-link attached by my nameless sliding knot, stopped by the bulk of the hooklength knot, is ample hardware for the terminal rig. In both cases, the leger should be the smallest needed to cast and to hold bottom.

The bite of a roach is gentle, and therefore the thinnest of quiver tips should be used. It may appear as a tremor lasting a second or two, or be one gentle tug. Anything resembling a bite should be studied, and certainly struck at if the tip stays in a pulled-round position. In a match situation, there have been times when I have struck at irregular intervals whether I have seen a bite or not, and it is surprising how many fish I have hooked in this manner, again an example of just how many bites we don't know about.

River roach of good size respond better to a piece of breadflake than any other bait I know. One piece squeezed on to a size 14–12 wide-gape hook is ideal, and though this may seem on the small side for big fish, it must be remembered that should a roach feel any weight whatsoever in the form of a hook, it will eject the bait in a flash. Reel line need be no more than 2.6lb with the hooklength at 1.7lb. Match anglers may go finer still in the effort to raise a bite, but take it from me, the difference of diameter and behaviour between the two lines is not noticed by the roach. With the legering method, it is even less obvious. However, the *behaviour* of the bait is of the utmost importance. If, for instance, a feeding fish attempts to suck the bait into its mouth, and the stiffness of the hooklength impairs the movement of the bait, it will be ignored.

Long ago, when on the Severn, my common practice was to put down a carpet of hempseed to attract a shoal of roach. If I knew the peg held a good head of roach I chucked in two pints at a time, perhaps once per hour over the course of a

Winter roaching. Counting maggots into a Drennan Feeder-Link.

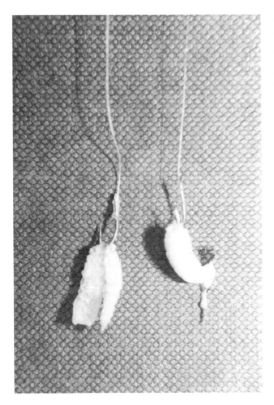

Roach will just nip the end of a maggot as in the single version. The double maggots have been sucked dry by a bream.

ues to this day. I either risk the refusal of my bait by roach because of stronger tackle, or face the possibility of losing barbel with roach gear. Fortunately, not all readers of this book will have similar problems, since barbel are not as well spread as roach.

STILLWATER ROACH

The chapter on bream contains much information which can be applied in the search for stillwater roach. The action of water mass, the movement of fish in various weather conditions – all can be applied in like form. After the basics have been sorted out, the similarities end, for the species are miles apart in the application of fishing techniques.

Strategy for an attack on stillwater roach depends on a number of factors. There should be a decent breeze; not a gale as fancied by many anglers, but enough air movement to put a far ripple on the surface with the light penetration, which roach dislike so much, reduced. Another factor is water colour. Following a good downpour, still water clouds up as mud and silt is washed from the banks; this can be assisted by underground inlets, be it stream or spring, all of which are conducive to good roach fishing.

In gravel pits especially, the onset of cooler weather puts roach into a feeding mood. Most pits are fed from underground springs, and as such can be affected by the surrounding area. Should it be arable farmland, then nitrates and other growth-promoting chemicals can do strange things. My local gravel pit at Upton Warren acts as a sailing centre as well as a very good fishery, and visiting sailors or anglers are wary of the strange colour, which is pea green at the best of times. This is certainly an algae growth, yet it has no detrimental affect on our fish – in fact, they thrive. Furthermore, there is no weed growth, a

five-hour match; the method attracted roach from well downstream and I enjoyed some successes. This was all very well until ·barbel were introduced into the river. It was quite disconcerting to hook a barbel of indeterminable size on a 1lb hooklength, and any form of massive feeding with hempseed produced the same result. I began to experiment. Without the use of hempseed, but with everything else aimed at roach, the same pattern was evident: a net of roach with a number of barbel. I now know that the two species live happily together, and the times I have played and landed 5–8lb barbel on roach tackle have been many – and hair raising. The dilemma contindirect result of the colour preventing growth-promoting sunlight; however, the pit is home to bream approaching ten pounds, big carp, tench which are rarely caught, roach over three pounds and hordes of crucians. During the colder months, Steve, Jake and I spend many days in the search of the big roach, and have learned a great deal about stillwater roach fishing. Like many pits, however, it changes from day to day, and still we learn, especially since nature has this nasty habit of breaking rules.

At about 3 a.m. one morning in May 1978, spending the night after eels at Westwood Park Great Lake, my attitude towards roach changed dramatically. Dreaming of a warm soft bed where bugs didn't bite, where rats and bats didn't squeak, I was brought to reality when a 50-pence piece balanced on the reel, fell from three feet to hit a car wheel dish. (This believe me, is better than a dozen high-tech. electronic bleepers sounding off together; *see* Chapter 12.) As the last vibes of the resounding 'clank' sent tremors far across the lake, I was at the butt, watching the coils fall slowly off the spool in the beam of the storm torch. I thought it came off much too slowly for an eel. Or was the eel running towards me, an experience I suffered the week previously? (On this occasion, having thought I had missed the bite, I reeled in loose line – only to find a lip-hooked 3lb eel almost crawling up the bank under my feet.)

No, this was different. It was more likely to be one of the big tench with which Westwood is so blessed. The passage of line stopped. Breathless minutes passed as I waited, my hand hovering over the butt. An eternity later I noticed the tiniest of movements as a further inch of line was taken. That was enough. Grabbing the rod, I struck mightily over my shoulder, taking the stretch of the 10lb line down to the two ounces of lead which lay far out into the lake. The rod, a purpose-built

2½lb test-curve eel-killer, hardly bent as a fish was hooked. No great fight was forthcoming, and less than a minute later a huge roach swam into the specimen landing-net. Four lobworms stuck on a size 2 eel hook hung from its mouth as would a spoonful of spaghetti, while the 15lb wire trace glistened in the beam of the torch.

That fish, at 2lb 14oz, my biggest roach to date at that time, had probably never seen a hook before. I felt betrayed. Following years in the search of a real humdinger of a specimen roach, using the finest of tackle and the freshest of baits, I had to catch it on eel tackle. That fish gave me no feeling of euphoria other than that I now knew roach of really specimen size lived in the Great Lake – and that they would eat a whole bunch of full-sized lobworms at night. Daytime, I'm afraid, was an entirely different matter.

During the following season I persevered with Westwood and its roach. Though I enjoyed the skills of float fishing, my favourite method was to leger at distance, with 2.6lb reel line tied direct to a ½oz bomb, using a size 14 hook to 1.7lb hooklength. With the use of a boat I discovered some good gravel beds, jotting down bankside references and distances. Sadly, and though catching many fine nets of fish, there was only one other Westwood roach which reached 2lb. That one sipped down a size 18 home-tied Greenwells Glory dry fly when I fished for stocked rainbow trout – foiled again!

I have caught but one roach over 3lb, which came from Upton Warren. A private pool had been netted and a number of roach to 3lb 12oz were put into the pit. They had probably been hand fed, for during the following months they were caught constantly. During a contest towards the end of the season, while taking indigenous roach and skimmers on the drop, I caught a splendid, very tame roach of 3lb 10oz. It was flawless.

11 Tench

Apart from carp, there are more devotees of the tench than perhaps any other stillwater fish. Such is their popularity that there is even an organization that meets on a regular basis to swap tales, ideas and methods, all to make it easier to catch specimen tench. Tench don't know this – but they are still difficult to catch at any time.

The tench is a fish seriously available for all-too-short a period. Following the first three months of the season they become harder to locate, more difficult to tempt, and by the time leaves begin to fall, they have all but disappeared. Predictably, most anglers forget them when September has passed.

Strangely, to catch small tench is rare. Personally, I have yet to catch one under 1½lb, but even at this relatively small size they are fine fighters who will test the mettle of both the angler and his tackle. Where the fry live and what they eat is a mystery. It is widely believed that small tench feed on daphnia and insect larvae such as bloodworm, etc. I have no doubt that this is true, yet ask any match angler if he has caught small tench in any quantity on his beloved bloodworm and the answer is always no (which is fine – who wants to catch small tench anyway?).

To find tench is easy: they live in lakes, gravel pits, slow rivers and canals all over the country. Vast tracts of water in Ireland are stuffed with tench, and with no close season in that country, the months of that period see anglers travelling from England by the thousand, many in search of big tench.

Once a venue is found, all that remains is to locate the fish, which again is not too difficult. At the beginning of the season, tench,

A nice size 'matchman's' tench.

more than any other stillwater fish, spread themselves all over lakes and gravel pits, moving constantly, stopping to feed a little before moving to other pastures. As they travel, small patches of bubbles are sent to the surface, created as the tench grub around, searching for food in the debris on the bed, and so telling anyone who may be remotely interested exactly where they are at any one time.

And that, my friends, is the end of the easy part of tench fishing. After this, the angler can find tench to be the most uncompromising, the most frustrating, infuriating fish that swims.

The six best tench I have taken at one sitting totalled 34lb 8oz, caught from Pearl Lake in Herefordshire on the first Monday of the season in 1991, a time which coincided with the middle of the heatwave. The water level was down to an all-time low, to the degree where the adjoining smaller lake was little more than a big puddle, yet both lakes remained home to 20lb carp, big tench and specimen roach.

I had participated in a small contest on the previous Sunday, catching four fish for 18lb – one on caster, two on sweetcorn, one on a huge lobworm – and losing a further four fish, certainly carp, for no tench on earth moved as fast as they.

The following day, the time of the *planned* assault, I commenced fishing at 6 a.m. Hours previously, in the glow of a moonlit night, I had rowed out in a borrowed boat. Once on the chosen station, I emptied two tins of sweetcorn, half a gallon of casters and countless scalded maggots over both sides, letting the boat drift gently to cover a wide area. Following this, I retired to the caravan for a well-earned sleep – not that it came easy.

A ghostly, early-morning mist obliterated the far bank as I set my tackle, yet not enough to prevent the sight of bubbles sent up by feeding tench. My tackle consisted of a home-made, soft-action eleven-foot rod of 1lb test curve, 3.2lb reel line direct to a size 12 hook, set at two feet from the lead-link, stopped by a multi-turn water knot. The link was 6in of line to a ½oz bomb. At length, absolutely bursting with anticipation, agog with excitement and with a piece of breadflake on the hook, I cast smack into the tench bubbles and fished. And fished some more. For over four hours I tried everything within reason without so much as a twitch. Yet bubbles continued to rise, some moving in a line as the tench grazed along the bed; the swim was stuffed with them. I tried all of the baits used in the groundbaiting exercise, all to no avail.

Ten o'clock had passed when my wife arrived with bacon sandwiches: a time to contemplate the bubbles, the failure, and last but not least, the delicious aroma of crisped pork. Then – a rare brainstorm. Reeling in, I squeezed a piece of bacon-flavoured bread on to the hook, casting with care to the baited area. Before the bait had time to reach the bottom the tip curved round as a fish intercepted the bread. I was 'in'.

It fought well, that first tench. After letting it run out of the swim, allowing me to do battle without upsetting the remainder of the shoal, I managed to slow it down, and so commenced a few minutes of the thumpety-thump fight of the tench, a curious musical count of four so seemingly common to tench I have caught. Fighting mad, around five pounds of solid muscle came to the shallows, the red eye glaring fiercely as I netted it. Five more followed, all taking the bacon-flavoured bread before the action stopped – as did the bubbles. Like anyone else who has caught a number of fish on a new bait, I though, 'Great, I've cracked it!' However, the life of the angler is, happily, not so simple. I have never since caught a tench or any other fish on bacon-flavoured bread.

During the remainder of that week I experimented with differing swims, arriving at the

A deeper, more shady corner where tench retire during a bright day.

following conclusions. Using the bubbles as a visual guide, I found that when the morning sun hits the water, tench move towards the source of the light, possibly looking for extra warmth. This search for a bit of comfort changes when the sun nears the zenith towards midday: the whole procedure turns around and tench seek more shaded areas, away from excessive heat and light. I believe this is a main reason for anglers to feel that the tench have 'gone off' – stopped feeding. If the angler has access to a lake where he can bait two swims, one of which remains in shade throughout the day, he will have more than a good chance of catching tench in the shaded one after the original swim has died.

Another peculiarity came to prominence in that big baits – worms, breadflake, etc. –

caught more fish during the early morning session, while particle baits – maggots, casters and sweetcorn – were far more productive during the daytime, but only in the shaded swim. As the latter baits were fished on thinner line and smaller hooks, I have no doubt this contributed to their success. Yet strangely, even when using a big bait on fine line and small hooks I did not get one single bite until the sun fell behind the trees on the far bank.

In May/June, tench go on a mad feeding spree, building up energy for the spawning which follows. This is the period when the biggest tench are caught, fat females so full of spawn that their bellies sag alarmingly when held for a photo. Though heavily pregnant, these fish will still fight well; but catch that same fish three months later and the angler

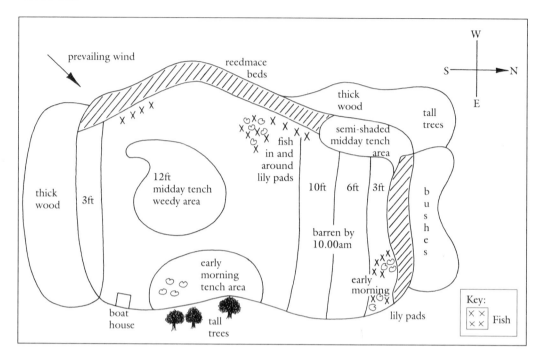

Fig. 21 Summer tench location on Westwood Lake.

will think it is three pounds heavier. To net a fit tench over 5lb safely, to witness the vibrant browny-green flanks, and to look straight into the blood-red eye must be one of the most satisfying feelings a fisherman can experience.

BAITS

Worms have always been my favourite bait for tench, and a single lobworm has accounted for 90 per cent of my total. However, Pearl Lake holds some good tench which take extremely kindly to small redworms, despite suffering a massive fish loss in the summer of 1990. This, I believe, is due to the amount of bloodworm in the lake; I can only describe them as a plague as there are literally millions of them. As such, the resident fish are very hard indeed to tempt on any bait except for

the smallest of redworms, especially in the warmer months when bloodworm are more plentiful.

Breadflake is also a superb tench bait. A thumbnail-sized piece squeezed on the shank of a size 10 hook has been the downfall of many a fine fish but, contrary to logical thought, masses of cloud groundbait which is normally used with flake can result in an empty swim. Following the cast, I like to flick a few dozen bits of rolled bread around the leger, assuming it is in flicking distance; if it is not, the use of a catapult is required. Should this be so, it's wise to wet the balls of bread to prevent them from flying off course.

Oxblood has always been recommended as a good attractor of tench, yet I have never witnessed anyone actually using it. I tried it just once, but to this day I have my suspicions whether or not the blood came from an ox. I planned a day on Westwood Lake, during the first week of the season in 1981. After consulting my local butcher, and after being treated in a terribly condescending manner, he smiled in a knowing way before promising me some oxblood. The following day I collected a half-gallon ice-cream container, full of dark, lumpy, disgusting blood, which I took home to mix with a gallon of dry crumb. The result was abominable: a smelly, sticky mush which took all of my willpower to look at, never mind touch. However, like all good anglers in search of 'the answers', I plucked up the courage to throw it in as groundbait. Predictably, the tench of Westwood Lake did not have an inkling that they were supposed to go utterly bonkers for this much publicized attractor, and in fact I think every fish within fifty yards disappeared fast.

Particle baits – anything small, numerous and edible – are very useful for tench. Maggots always have their day, as does sweetcorn, but on all waters where I have caught tench, casters have been more productive as regards both size and quantity of fish. Various nuts are also useful, but I think unnecessary unless the venue has been fished to death for carp.

Methods

Many aspects of location pertaining to bream can be applied also to tench, but there is one glaring difference in that tench much prefer weeded areas. If a tench water has but one weed bed in it, that is where the tench will be, and if the water has many weed beds, the edge of the thickest, most dense area is the place to fish.

Just about every book I have read on tench, without exception, repeats one passage constantly: the vital need to rake a tench swim beforehand. This may be true for those who have stated so, but I must confess it has never worked for me. Any tench I have caught have been the result of trying to locate the fish and feeding the swim, not by raking up a mess of mud and bubbles hoping some tench will come along and stay there. In fact, I was thrown off one water for doing just that.

The lake was on a private estate near Oxford; it was expensive to fish, difficult to find, yet reputedly worth every penny. After arriving, and being shown the best swims by the water bailiff – a most charming gentleman – I set my tackle and threw in my two-foot wide, double-sided home-made rake, tied to a length of rope. The resulting splash brought back our friend the bailiff who, showing distinct signs of an apoplectic fit, cussed and raved as I pulled in a mass of weed. I was asked to leave the water immediately, never to return. Though hurt at the time, I could later do little but agree with his views. If every tench angler on that lake had removed every piece of weed in every swim there would have been very little weed left anywhere, never mind leaving the banks covered in rotting, smelly, fly-infested rubbish. The smooth silkweed which grows on the beds of many stillwaters is another matter altogether. If this can be gently stirred up, releasing the tiny bugs and insects which live in and under it, then it's quite possible that any passing tench will stop to eat them. In respect of swim dragging, or weed displacement, I think we must, therefore, be very wary of ancient methods (and irate bailiffs!).

At the beginning of the season, when the angler sets stall on a known tench lake, he should look for swims that are close to weed or covered banks. Later into the season, tench become less nomadic, and will be found in the deeper areas away from the bank during daylight hours. The bubbles, as mentioned previously, will show if any tench are in residence and, again, this is time for the binoculars.

One happy habit of tench is that when the angler is using big baits, say lobworm or breadflake, they do not mess about. When a tench takes such a bait the angler knows it, and no matter what is used as a bite indicator, the positive bite leaves little to doubt.

Maggots are another matter altogether. At times, bite indication may be so delicate that it might appear as though a minnow is playing with the bait. I have a subconscious picture of a fickle tench which seems to pick one up, hold it between its lips for ages before dropping it again, perhaps to poke it around the bed for a while before repeating the process. Maybe I'm not too far from fact. Casters are a much better bet. Not only will tench take them with greater confidence, but casters stay in one spot after they have been put into the swim; they don't wriggle away to safety. Maggots which have been scalded can be used, but are not in the same league as a carpet of casters.

When using small baits such as maggots, casters or sweetcorn, the angler must be on his toes, unlike fishing for bream, where the golden rule is to let the bite develop. I am greatly in favour of holding the rod at all times when tenching, striking at any movement of line, tip or whatever form of indication I am using. Just occasionally, the bite may be easy to see, and occasionally easy to connect with. On a hard-fished water, however, after having numerous hooks stuck in their mouths, they become more finicky, dropping a bait if they sense that all is not well. In these instances, to tackle up with a lighter set-up all round is a good bet. A softer rod can be balanced with lighter line and a smaller hook, resulting in more natural presentation.

On venues that contain carp, tench, to the utter annoyance of the carp anglers, are hooked too many times. No carp man who has sat behind his array of rods for a week or more wants to see a red-eyed tench in his landing-net, but he has no easy answer to his problem; whatever bait or method he may use, tench could move into his swim in quantity. The tench man, however, is faced with a very enjoyable situation here, for to catch tench to the exclusion of carp requires even more thought, and a lot of luck. Now, he wouldn't *mind* a carp or two taking his bait!

As always, the swimfeeder is used more than anything else by tench anglers. Though I am a great believer that groundbait can be counter-productive to continuous good tench fishing, an open-end feeder, filled with brown crumb and laced with hookbait samples such as casters, maggots, sweetcorn, etc. is a method which will certainly catch odd tench. A medium blockend, however, filled with maggots only is more productive, keeping a shoal of tench in the swim for a longer period.

The method works much better later in the season when tench are more difficult to come by. It is again a matter of casting constantly to the same area – not necessarily the same spot, for as in bream fishing, a shoal of tench cover a wide area. A reel line of 5lb is ample, with the hook tied direct, and with this strong tackle the angler should have every chance to land any tench he may encounter. The feeder can be attached to a bead or swivel if so desired, though a simple water knot/sliding line arrangement will suffice quite well. The distance from hook to link can be varied occasionally to give a different presentation, 18in being a nice average to start with. If any flicker of interest is shown without full development, this can be increased to 3ft.

The use of the feeder in a heavily weeded lake or pit is asking for trouble, for weed in a shallow, spring-fed lake, one which is subject to heavy chemical influx from farmland, can grow to the surface. Westwood is one such lake, from where I have pulled weed over ten feet high. Also, there are many lakes which are too shallow to use a feeder effectively. In these situations, the straight leger is a much safer bet, if only to eliminate the loud splash of the feeder, which can alarm feeding fish.

The leger should be as light as is required to cast to the chosen area, which, in the case of shallow lakes, can lead to difficulties in sinking the line. The best way to overcome this is to remove the spool from the reel, leaving it to soak overnight in warm water containing just a spot of washing-up liquid; the line will then sink like the proverbial stone. Thinner, more presentable line can be used with a straight leger; using a soft-action ten-to eleven-foot rod you will find 3.2lb b/s is ample, again going direct to the hook. When fishing close to a weed-free, shallow bank, 2.6lb line is much more fun, and quite safe.

I must confess to having doubts as to the supposed necessity of strong lines for still-water fish; this probably stems from my matchfishing days, but I can only remark on my own experiences. For years we have read of anglers using lines of 6–8lb in search of stillwater fish yet, carp and eels apart, I cannot envisage any other species that requires such strong tackle. These days high-tech rods, most of which have a computer-measured test curve, make silly the use of 8lb line on a 1½lb test-curve rod. With tench second only to carp in strength, and nowhere near them in size or weight, I believe that line over 5lb b/s is unbalanced in relation to the job it has to do. Anything stronger would be like using hawser cable to tow a mini.

There was one occasion, however, when things got out of hand. On Westwood, I was catching roach under the rod end when a much larger fish took the single caster bait, tearing off to the centre of the sixty-acre lake. The twelve-foot glass float rod coped well, and eventually a tench came to the net. All I had was a rather rusty set of 14lb Little Sampson scales, which registered at just over 7lb, which I thought was not a bad fish considering I was using a size 20 hook to 1lb hooklength. The fish gave me the fight of my life, making a wonderful addition to my net of roach. Later at home, I tested the scales with an unopened bag of sugar. They were weighing 8–10oz over the top. It was still a good fish.

Tench, in general terms, again like bream, respond well to a change bait method. After catching one or two and then finding the fish have 'gone off', a change of bait can sometimes do the trick, and the change from, say, worm to flake to maggot to worm again may turn up a single fish per change. On the other hand, a change can at times result in a string of bites; in this respect, tench are like trout, switching from one bait to another without apparent reason.

The use of particle baits needs a groundbaiting plan which, in the case of some anglers, can reach almost saturation point. Gallons of maggots are often used, which in a gravel pit results in most of them crawling under the gravel, unless they are scalded first and so stay put. Pint after pint of casters are thrown in, which is fine if there are enough hungry tench there to eat them all. The chances are that stunted roach, perch, gudgeon and all sorts will invade the swim first. Far better, I would think, to encourage tench into the swim in the first place. The smallest amount of groundbait, say half a pint (soaked in oxblood if the angler is so inclined) can be laced with a few juicy items such as sweetcorn, worms, and perhaps a few rolled bits of bread. Once the tench are obviously in evidence, and hopefully feeding, *then* the mass particle attack can be put into operation.

Particle feeding techniques are based on the fish becoming addicted to whatever is being used at the time. Hempseed, sweetcorn, maggots, casters, etc. are all very good on the day. The problem is that tench, after eating one, do not move very far to find the next morsel, and when the hookbait is taken the bite indication can be next to nothing. When faced with this problem, it's wise to shorten the hooklength to an inch if necessary. In this manner, the fish will only have to turn its head to give bite indication, when the angler needs to time his strike to perfection. Should the tench feel any resistance it will eject the hookbait in a flash.

Hooksize is, of course, relative to the bait. Should it be particles, then sizes 18–14 will cover all requirements, with perhaps a size 12 to accommodate doubles of sweetcorn, a medium-sized worm, or multiple maggots or casters. Lobworms or breadflake will need hooks up to size 6, preferably with a wide gape to facilitate easy hooking, and if the angler is into the secret world of boilies he can use a hook which can be buried.

The night fisherman will find the use of optonics and visual bite indicators mandatory, but I have reservations of this being the best time for tench fishing. Late evening, perhaps an hour into darkness, and the first three hours of daylight are by far the best times.

The Hair Rig

Modern-day techniques are fast approaching the time when the poor old fish, tench included, will have no option whatsoever in being hooked, for modern rigs are based on persuading a fish to take a bait which does not have a hook in it! The 'hair rig' is a hook/bait arrangement designed by carp anglers, and while it is certainly effective in fooling the odd carp, it seems to fool tench even more. The bait, usually a boilie, is attached to a separate piece of fine line next door to the hook, and hopefully, the fish, finding nothing in the bait to alarm it, eats it. By this time it's too late for the fish, the hook is either in its mouth or alongside its jaw; as it moves off – still unaware – the angler sees the bite indication and smacks the hook home, sometimes on the outside of the mouth. A hair is made from a short length of Kryston, or Dacron, lines manufactured from braided thread-like fibres which are tremendously strong for the given diameter, but it is the limpness factor which is all important: a fish picking up a bait feels no resistance whatsoever other than the natural weight of the bait. Nylon line of 1.1lb b/s is equally as good. A tiny loop is tied into the end of the hair, and the hair is then pulled through the bait with a baiting needle. The hair is now wrapped around the hook, leaving enough to position the bait alongside the hook. A device to prevent the bait from falling off during the cast is required, and though there are purpose-made 'stoppers' available, a piece of thick nylon line ¼in long will suffice, slipped into the loop before being pulled into the bait. While this basic form of hair rig would make many a specimen hunter shudder in its simplicity, it is quite adequate.

As with many fish, tench respond quite favourably to a pre-baiting programme. A daily dose of particle baits in a couple of swims over a period of a few days will soon have tench in residence, though it's unwise to pile in masses of cereal groundbait. Sweetcorn and hempseed are attractor baits which will not bury themselves under silt or gravel, while casters are also very good; maggots should be scalded to prevent them disappearing.

I am aware that this chapter has passages which appear to argue with each other. Perhaps this is how it should be, for the habits of tench change in like manner, and no advice or book can provide answers to their unique behaviour. Happily, that sixth, most important sense of all comes with experience; it falls into place quite quickly, but an angler new to tench fishing can suffer it all through one entire season. During this time, he will fish for the tench in all of their unpredictable moods, suffering blanks and having those wonderfully rare rod-bending days. There is nothing quite like it.

12 Eels

Let me say at the outset of this chapter that I do not consider myself a great catcher of eels. In fact, the sight of one makes my stomach churn, yet at the same time I can understand the fascination eels generate in their thousands of followers. The most dedicated eel man I have known was the late John Sidley. During the summer of 1979 I was privileged to spend one or two nights eeling in the company of John, occasions when I learned a great deal, for which I am grateful. In the years which have followed I have seen no great improvements in eel-fishing techniques.

Eel fishing is essentially a night-time occupation. Though many anglers, in particular specimen hunters, are loners by nature, I would suggest the most sensible thing anyone can do is to go eel fishing with at least one partner. In my time I have engaged in a bit of nocturnal fishing and, believe me, no matter how strong a man's will, at 3 a.m. his mind will play tricks. Little bugs become tarantulas, lovable dormice are suddenly kingsize rabid rats, and the swish of a tree swaying in a breeze could be an escaped gorilla from the local Safari Park. However, in spite of the foregoing mental horrors, night fishing will always have its disciples.

More than anything else which swims, eels are a fish of the night. They follow the strange pattern of certain fish who prefer to smell out their food. Once winter has passed and waters begin to warm, is it time to think of eeling,

and there can be no better conditions than a sultry night in June. If a thunderstorm is forecast, so much the better. The oppressive atmosphere, heavy with expectation, plays a large part in the conditions *under* the water, encouraging eels from their lairs to forage in a most accommodating fashion, and if the angler can plan his trip accordingly and chooses a night without moon, with thunder rolling across the heavens, rain lashing down and lightning illuminating lake and tree, and although almost certain to become half drowned in the process, he will have a wonderful chance of catching eels.

TACKLE

There is no room for finesse in eeling. A rod capable of landing a 40lb pike is admirable, the strong reel filled with line of no less than 10lb b/s, and a lot of it. A standard Arlesey bomb of 1½–2oz will be adequate, tied to a free-running swivel, stopped at least 3ft from the hook.

Opinions differ on the properties of the hooklength. I am greatly in favour of using a simple wire trace, for eels have a nasty habit of biting through nylon line no matter how strong. Yet there are excellent eel anglers who swear that wire kinks terribly when an eel is hooked, rendering it useless thereafter. I have never experienced this, but even should it be so, I would much sooner be forced to change my hooklength many times than chance having eel after eel bite its way free.

A trace can be purchased complete with swivels and snap-link for hook attachment, or the angler can make his own. Wire trace, or alasticum as it is known, can be purchased in bulk form, and I would suggest nothing less than 15lb b/s. A packet of strong size 2 eyed hooks are needed, a Drennan Starpoint being ideal. The micro-barb of this hook enables it to be removed much more easily, using a pair of good forceps, for to shift any hook from the vice-like mouth of a good eel is difficult at the best of times.

To make up a trace is simple. The wire is passed through the eye twice, then wound around itself many times – at least a dozen – and finished off with a tuck at the top end before pulling tight; the swivel attachment is formed in a similar fashion, and I can assure you that nothing will come adrift in the form of unravelling, though a totally dedicated eel man will finish the bind with either a crimp or a dab of solder. It's wise to make up a number of traces before going fishing, wrapping each trace around a piece of stiff cardboard for safety, or even using a pole-rig winder.

There is no need to consider balance of lead to depth or distance; in fact, I believe it is wise to go a little on the heavy side. The strong rod, with the strong line will cast a 2oz bomb out of sight. The suggested weight of Arlesey bomb is ideal for most situations, tied to a 6in link, but this link will be variable, depending on other factors such as depth of bottom weed, or whether the bait is to be suspended on top of the weed.

The use of two swivels is paramount. A decent size of good quality is needed, for the eel, which can take a bait with surprising delicacy, goes completely livid once hooked, wriggling, twisting and performing every underwater gyration imaginable to free itself.

BAITS

There is no need for extensive debate here, as there are but two serious eel baits to consider: lobworms and small dead fish. A great number of lobworms can be used during a single night, for the technique demands that up to four are put on the hook each time. As many specialist eel catchers fish for days on end, it will be appreciated that a worm hunt of extensive proportions is required and hundreds need to be collected. A deep bucket full of damp moss will keep them fresh, hardening them too, which is necessary when a long cast is performed.

A small roach or other silver fish (as compared with a drab gudgeon) of around two to four inches is ideal for eeling. In these days of conservation, however, the angler must be extremely careful as to where he gets his dead baits from, for the spread of disease is all too common. Many owners of waters will be rightly upset if fish from other venues are used for eeling, so I would advise any deadbait be appropriated from the fishery concerned, if possible.

Eels will of course eat other food, and the small 'bootlace' youngsters become nuisance fish to the users of maggots. Unless the angler is lightning fast with his strike, they almost always swallow the hook. These little eels are covered in a thick mucus, which makes a terrible mess of landing-nets, line and clothes too, if the angler is careless, and they should be handled most carefully, if at all. Far better to cut the trace above the hook and tackle up again.

If the prospective eel angler has access to a boat, he can pre-bait the chosen area with all sorts of rubbish, creating a form of freshwater rubby-dubby as used by shark anglers: bits of meat, chopped worms, chopped fish, etc. This should be carried out a few hours before the session, covering a large area, allowing the eels to follow the scent from many corners of the lake. As I have already said, no stillwater is completely still, and the scents from the loose-fed baits will attract eels from far away.

METHODS

The first essential of any night fishing is to be organized before darkness falls. Tackle not required should be stored out of harm's way, while baits, nets and other necessary items should be at hand. Adequate clothing, though perhaps not needed, should always be taken for emergency purposes. A good storm torch is a must, positioned to shine on the butt area of the rod, while a hand torch is also a necessity.

A really high-profile eel angler will be housed in a bivouac, complete with a collapsible bed-chair. He will possess a gas stove, micro-fridge, mini-television, tins of anything edible, recipe book, and – if there is room – a sink and a washing line. He may even have a communication method. One night, while working my spaniel around Westwood Lake, I came across an angler talking to his mate at the far end of the dam wall through an army walkie-talkie set, complete with regimental emblems, and even as I listened I heard a detailed discussion of wives who nagged, the price of beer, and a much briefer talk of tactics, baits and the effects of wind direction.

The double rod-rest set-up is mandatory when eeling, with the rear rest positioned where the angler can reach it without smashing his tackle all over the place. More than anything, the casting position should be carefully considered; an angler must watch for the possibility of fouling overhanging branches, or hooking a bush close behind – in short, he should choose a peg with plenty of room.

To cast to the same area during the darkness of night demands a sixth sense common to the experienced night angler. He will put just the right amount of power into the rod each time, freeing the line at the right moment, sending the terminal rig to near enough the same area each time. The search for eels, however, does not require the same degree of casting accuracy as for bream or tench. If no rubby-dubby has been put in, then it makes good sense to cast to different areas in search of the fish.

The numerous optonic bite indicators on the market, are unnecessary when eeling, and anyway, for the life of me I can see no justification in these prices. Thankfully, my friend John Sidley put paid to my taking out a second mortgage. Once the cast is made, and the terminal tackle straightened out, the rod is put in the rests. Any slack line is taken in, and the bale arm is opened into the casting position, after which a coin such as an old 10-pence piece is placed on top of the spool, trapping the line. A 'bobbin' such as a bit of mud will have enough weight to hold the line down, after which a metal wheel disc is placed directly under the reel; the lid of a biscuit tin will also suffice, though this does not achieve such a spectacular result. When a fish takes the bait, the mud is jerked up and off and the line is pulled from the spool, moving the coin. The results are positive. At 3 a.m., the angler, perhaps fast asleep and knee-deep in a land of ten-foot long eels, will, when the coin hits the metal, awake thinking the Third World War has begun.

Worms are mounted on the hook in threes or fours, broken in half, the whole mess ending up looking something like a small octopus. This in itself may be no coincidence, for the larger sea-going conger eels, no doubt closely associated with the freshwater species, must eat small octopuses in great numbers. Also, the juices from the worm, which eels find so delicious, are released, so adding to the attraction of the bait.

Coin on spool bite indicator.

A longer lead-link may be required if the bottom is heavily weeded. This will allow the bunch of worms to have a chance of settling in a loose fashion, where to be hung tight into a thick weed would be to have no chance whatsoever of a continuous take. At certain times, eels will take a bait from the top of such weed, and an injection of air is administered to the worm to make it semi-buoyant. Any old syringe will suffice for this, though purpose-made models are available from specialist suppliers.

A small roach or bream is ideal for an eel bait. The fish must then be mounted correctly. The first thing to do is to attach the lead-link, sliding the swivel up the line and out of

A bunch of worms is the greatest of eel baits.

the way. Using a baiting needle, the reel line is then threaded through the tail end of the fish, and out at the mouth. The trace is now attached, and when secure, pulled into the fish, out the other end, leaving the hook point *outside* the mouth; to prevent the fish from sliding up the line, a swan shot can be nipped on at the point where the trace emerges from the tail end. The lead-link swivel is stopped with a small shot which rests on top of the trace knot, leaving the link to slide freely. The swim bladder of the deadbait should be pierced with a knife or it may float. Should the swim be weedy, though, this buoyancy can be taken advantage of as the bait will lie semi-suspended on top of the weed.

The bite of an eel is unlike any other fish. It picks up the bait and moves a foot, only to stop and taste a bit more, before moving again, a pattern which varies in repetition. I don't think this has anything to do with inde-cision, for should that be so it would drop the bait at the first inkling of danger. This, I believe, is the natural way in which an eel takes food, a stop/start pattern which is com-mon to the species. At all times, the angler must wait for the eel to eat the bait, moving off as it does, resulting in the aptly termed 'run'. Even so, I missed dozens of eel runs in the times I fished seriously for them. I tried different time lapses, waiting for the run to develop, or attempted to connect with the bite at the first movement of the line. My con-clusions are that eels, similar to other fish, take food as they see fit at any given time. Much as we humans demand exquisite pre-sentation of our meals when faced with silver service in the best of hotels, while in a more relaxed mood, we will pick fish and chips from paper with relish.

I have no doubt that in many cases, the misses are a result of the eel moving towards the fishing position. Even when using a hefty lead, the best that can happen is for the lead to hold fast enough to put just a little pressure on the hook, when an eel with any modicum of self-preservation will drop it instantly. Hap-pily, more often than not, the eel will take the bait outwards or sideways, and the strike will connect quite well.

When night fishing for eels, there are prob-lems over which the angler has no control. Just about every fish which swims likes worms, and over a period of time the angler can expect to catch every species which may be in the fishery. I have already related the tale of my favourite Westwood roach. Tench to over 5lb have also come to the net, roach/bream hybrids to 4lb, perch by the dozen, while my long-time angling mate Bob Jones once netted a pike of 22lb which chomped with gusto at his six-lobworm set-up.

My strangest catch ever was a very irate, very noisy pure white duck – one which enjoyed diving to six feet to find worms! It fought as no fish ever could inasmuch it insist-ed on taking off many times before crashing to the water once more. That poor duck had no chance whatsoever of escape when hooked on eel tackle, and once netted went berserk as I removed the hook before returning it to the water, one would hope a much wiser duck.

The angler may not know what sort of fish he may have hooked in certain instances, but once he has hooked his first eel he will be left in no doubt. The fight of a good-sized eel is unique in the fact that it doesn't really go any-where. It tugs and jerks as it twists, as though it is yanking its head from one side to the other, swimming backwards, sideways for one foot, then as much the other way. There is no powerful surge as with carp or barbel, no dogged run for bankside roots as with chub – but what it can do, very well indeed, is to hook its tail around anything it can find. When an eel of any size manages to do this, it becomes a matter of who will win the tug of war. On most occasions I would back the eel.

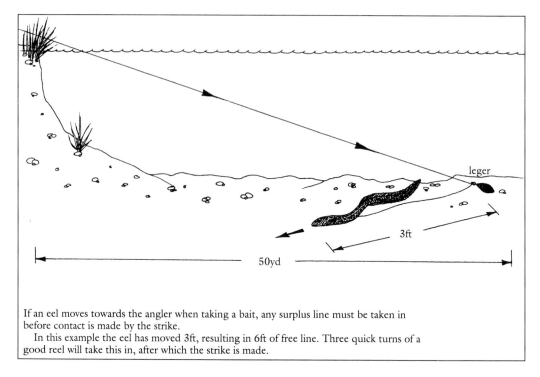

leger

3ft

50yd

If an eel moves towards the angler when taking a bait, any surplus line must be taken in
before contact is made by the strike.

In this example the eel has moved 3ft, resulting in 6ft of free line. Three quick turns of a
good reel will take this in, after which the strike is made.

Fig. 22 A common eel run.

Many years ago I took my family for a week-long holiday to the famous Llangorse Lake near the Brecon Beacons in mid-Wales. A small stream ran off the lake, spanned by a tiny footbridge, a stream no more than a few inches deep. One particular day, I came upon Steve and Jake lying over the parapet of the bridge, attempting to remove a sheet of corrugated iron half buried in the stream. They told me they had seen a fish swim under, I thought perhaps one of the many dabs with which the stream was stuffed. Lying with them, I watched for a while. Slowly, the head section of an eel came into view, just a few inches of it, enough to see it was of quite broad girth. A little more came out, the head moving from side to side as it scanned the area, until one of the lads moved, when it withdrew quickly.

Like all good holiday-makers, we had purchased a crab line, the round bobbled leger tied to orange line of at least 50lb b/s, with a hook big enough to anchor a battleship. Finding a worm from the soft bankside earth, I lowered it to the edge of the metal sheet, dangling it at the entrance to the bolt hole of the eel. It took just that one instance to get the eel to shoot out like a rocket, snatching the worm, pulling it under the sheet amid a spurt of muddy water. I will never know the size of that eel, but I do know it had the strength of a devil and the tenacity of a bulldog. I pulled, heaved, even tied the line to my wrist and walked backwards. At length, pity overcame my fighting spirit and I cut the line as it went under the sheet. I never forgot that incident, and during those eeling sessions at Westwood I allowed not one eel to reach for the bottom.

It's good fun to pump in a big eel, and extremely satisfying to net it in the specimen-sized landing-net. But oh dear me, what a mess. The mucus of the eel is all but immovable: it clings to clothes and nets like glue. When removing an eel from the net, it's wise to use a good-sized towel (disposable) to grip it, holding it tightly to remove the hook with forceps. A clout with a heavy object on the position of the vent is supposed to stun an eel, though in my experience that sends it into an even more vicious paroxysm of rage.

There is a supposedly holy mediaeval belief that to lay an eel within the long arm of a worshipful cross, scraped from the ground, will render it immobile, after which it will lie supine in this divine cradle. This, holy or not, is an old wives' tale – it will writhe out in an instant. There are but two actions to consider: it can be netted for day-time photos, or dispatched for eating purposes by the humane method of cutting off its head.

The conservation factor is null and void in the context of the eel. The tiny larvae leave the Sargasso Sea in multi-billions, drifting with time and tide. They take up to two years to reach estuaries, by which time they have grown to 2in in length, and are now called elvers. During this journey they are plundered by everything which swims, including sea birds. Those who survive this decimation enter the rivers only to be netted by the hundredweight by man, yet thousands remain to continue the species, wriggling overland into every type of water they can find, from river to pond, from canal to drinking-supply reservoir. So, should the occasion arise when you want to get into the will of a very rich great aunt who much enjoys a jellied eel or two, take them without fear – there must be a million left for every one eaten.

Prepared for an all-night session.

13 Carp

The most dedicated carp anglers – most far more expert than myself – have, over decades, written books relating successful methods, consequent joys and heart-rending failures. Many have made carp the reason for living, and so I must tread very carefully as I encroach into such kingly territory. Suffice, I think, just to touch on the very basics, which I hope will be enough to whet the appetites of any budding specimen carp hunters.

On our gravel pit at Upton Warren we catch carp no more than a foot from the bank, and to be frank they are not very difficult. Walking around the margins, it's easy to spot a fish grubbing at the bottom, the tail dark but visible in the green water as

A boilie-caught mirror carp from Upton Warren, hooked at 12 noon in high sun. About 14lb.

the carp stands almost on its head. A bait, be it meat, bread, sweetcorn or a bunch of maggots, is weighted with a swan shot and lowered gently into the swim a yard in front of the direction the fish is taking. Most times the bait is ignored, but just now and again the carp is fooled and tears off to the middle of the pit, so commencing the rip-roaring antics of a well-hooked good carp. Seven-pound fish are plentiful, a double is not unknown, with a 15lb mirror always on the cards. No shades of Savay or Redmire, it is still great fun.

BAITS

Carp are almost force fed as far as baits are concerned, for this is an industry on its own. Boilies, that quaint term applied to the little balls of boiled rusk and whisked egg supplemented with anything which smells, have been around for over a decade, accounting for, I would think, 99.9 per cent of all carp caught. The additives are too many to mention here, but they must run into hundreds, if not thousands. Tutti-Frutti, Bird-food, Fishmeal, Aniseed, Mango, Green-Lipped Mussel, Passion Fruit and Garlic are all successful flavourings and may give some indication of the vast range.

Domestic science is helpful with boilie manufacture. Should the angler require something different, they can be put into a microwave oven for a minute or so, which dehydrates them, thus making them buoyant. This is the 'pop-up' boilie, a bait which can be suspended at any depth that the angler chooses. But it is my duty

here to warn of problems. Certain additives or flavours, such as fishmeal or garlic will – in seconds – fill the house with the most disgusting smell imaginable. The best idea I can think of is to use an extension lead, take the microwave to the bottom of the garden and do the business in peace. Sadly, the appliance will need fumigating afterwards.

Nuts too are used in great quantities. Once more, there is a seemingly endless list of them which, along with hempseed, sweetcorn and others, come into the category of particle baits. Carp love particle baits as do roach, gudgeon, bream and tench. I would advise, therefore, that the angler is very careful as to where he puts his particles.

There is one glaring fact which many carp anglers, more so those new to the game, tend to forget. The aforementioned high-tech. baits, which are necessary on notoriously hard waters, may be next to useless on carp waters which have been little fished. On such venues the angler need look no further than plain old bread, meat, worms, cheese and sweetcorn to catch his carp, for they will find these tasty baits

An anorexic common of 4lb. It was caught in 6 inches of water next to the keep net.

A few of the many additives with which hookbaits are treated, including maggots, worms, sweetcorn and boilies.

angler will take the whole business much further. He may use a boilie launcher, a device which can be loaded with a thousand boilies, sending them out one after the other. Another method is to purchase a radio-controlled boat which can be directed to any point on any lake before the signal to 'unload' is transmitted, when the servos operate to dump the baits – usually particles, thousands of them – into the swim. (I once saw an angler carefully assemble a terminal tackle on to one of these boats, sending it to a pre-baited area, giving line by hand from his reel before pressing the button to unload. He carried this out three times with three different sets of tackle, carefully setting the audible bite indicators. Then, after zipping himself into his bivvy, he fell asleep.)

Above all other fish, the carp responds to pre-baiting a swim; in fact, on hard-fished venues pre-baiting is almost mandatory. It is not uncommon to chuck in hundreds of boilies daily which, when supplemented with a variety of nuts and particle baits, provide the carp with a permanent larder. The idea is, of course, to attract carp into the swim, to keep them there and to lull them into believing all baits are safe. Then, after a week or two of pre-baiting, the golden day arrives when the lulled carp takes the bait with the hook in it, hopefully with gay abandon.

much to their liking. Nor will he need to master the many weird and wonderful rigs; a strong line using a simple running leger will be adequate. Once treated to a full season of boilie baiting, however, carp will be addicted, and infinitely more difficult to tempt. To a lesser degree, so will many other coarse fish.

The attractor baits can be introduced by hand or catapult, but the dedicated carp

Could you lend me your glasses?

TACKLE AND METHODS

Tackle must, of course, be strong. To emulate the record 51lb fish as caught by Chris Yates may be beyond the hopes of most carp anglers, the main reason being that they simply do not have access to venues which hold fish of such proportions. However, most carp waters have fish which will bend the strongest of carp rods, and in waters where carp reach over 20lb a rod with a test curve of 2lb is needed. Line should not be less than 10lb using a reel capable of holding 200 yards. There are purpose-made carp hooks available, obviously strong, and once again the whole secret is balance, to match the size of the hook to the bait used. An eyed Drennan Starpoint size 12 would be fine for a couple of grains of sweetcorn, while a size 4 would not be out of place using bread or meat. Though using an eyed hook, a standard hook-tie knot is the strongest, threading the line through the eye before tying the knot. The line then tightens on to itself, eliminating further damage which may be caused by the metal of the eye.

In any form of fishing I believe simplicity should be applied whenever possible, and even more so when it comes to terminal rigs. In the case of a normal carp water, where the carp do not have 'A' levels in hook detection, a simple running swivel-link will be quite satisfactory, stopped with a small shot after tying in a multi-turn water knot. Hooklengths as usual are a matter of experimenting until hittable bites develop, though not to silly extremes either way. An 18in hooklength to a 4in swivel link is worth a try to begin with.

Explanations of specialist terminal rigs would take up half of this book, and even should I have the room, I would hesitate to recommend some of them, for in my view they are wondrously over-complicated; but then I am no dedicated carp angler. I have no doubt that the inventors of such rigs firmly believe they are conducive to the catching of carp, and as such become more confident.

The hair-rig system as mentioned in Chapter 11 is mandatory in advanced carp techniques, as is the helicopter rig and the nefarious bolt rig, plus a host of other ploys. There is also a myriad of smaller items to consider, from anti-tangle rubbers to fast-release boom connectors, many of which are developed with conservation in mind, and can only be applauded. Others have but one job to do: they are invented to fool carp. I firmly believe that many fool anglers even more.

A form of groundbaiting invented by carp anglers is quaintly termed a 'stringer'. A number of boilies, or whatever hookbait is being used, is threaded on to a length of soluble string and tied to the terminal tackle in the region of the hook. The casting technique must be adjusted to heave out the extra bulk, but the end result is well worth the trouble. After a short while in the water the string melts, leaving the samples entirely free from any encumbrance. (I have since experimented on barbel with this technique using meat, with great success.)

The continuance of the metal industry must owe a great deal to carp anglers, for the vast array of rod-rests, buzzbars, etc. is big business indeed, and no serious carp angler should skimp in this area. Up to three rods at a time are used, all matched, as are the reels, which sit on a rest, set-up in a very imposing manner. Three audible bite indicators are included in this system, adjusted against wind, currents, or anything else which may give rise to a carpless bleep. Included in the bite registration set-up is the modern-day bobbin replacement entitled a 'monkey climber', a brightly coloured object attached to the reel line by an instant-release clip between the reel and first butt rig. This rises as a fish takes line, and when the strike is made, falls from the reel line having done its job. (Though looking extremely professional, and in full knowledge that carp anglers are fast movers, I often wonder what would happen if three carp all took a bait at the same time.)

A specimen-sized landing-net is obviously required, though to put a big carp in a keepnet is considered an act of heresy. To keep carp captive for any length of time, a purpose-made 'carp sack' is used, in which the carp will lie quiet, safe and completely unharmed for a short period. With conservation high in the priorities of all anglers, to let a specimen carp – or any other big fish for that matter – lie on hard earth, be it gravel,

This angler is using two matched rigs for carp with the third rod using a luminous float in the shallows of the near bank. The 'miners' hat light leaves his hands free.

harsh grass or whatever, can do harm as this removes the protective mucus and scales. The world of carp has developed a special item for this in the 'unhooking mat', upon which the fish can be safely laid as the hook is carefully removed. Carp anglers are, in my opinion, the most conservation minded of all. Other branches of the sport could do well to follow their example.

For the record, the budding carp man will need to keep a diary. These can be purchased ready-made for the angler, with boxes where he can record wind directions and speeds, temperatures of air and water, depths fished, baits used, total man hours per rod/per day/per week; and – if any – fish caught, the name (Flecked Fred, Ginny with the Light Brown Fin, Ole Torn-Tail, Big Bum, etc.) plus its weight this time, last time and anything else which might just be applicable next time.

LOCATION

Location of carp is almost a science. This is where binoculars and polaroids come into use, for to search the surface of lake or pit looking for carp that roll is a big part of the carp angler's day. Once he sees a fish break the surface regularly at one spot he has accomplished something vital: he positively knows where a fish is. Whether or not he eventually hooks that fish is another matter entirely, but it's very nice to know you are at least casting to an area where a carp is in residence, much better I think than hoping one will come along. The binoculars can also be used to see the clouds of bubbles sent to the surface by carp grubbing around on the bottom, much as the bream angler will look for a patch of muddy water.

On big waters, an echo sounder is a must to help map out underwater contours, deep holes, bars of gravel or long shallow arms which

A young Jake Lees with his very first match win with 31lb of crucians from Upton Warren gravel pit. John Sherwood is in attendance.

stretch out into gravel pits, all giving the knowledgeable carp angler an indication of where he may – or may not – locate fish. It would take a number of outings on a boat to map out a chart, though the effort would be well worth the trouble. Wind direction plays a large part in where carp may be found, and one factor to bear in mind is that carp will favour a downwind bank in any lake or pit.

Though widely believed to be a fish of the summer, it is known that carp feed well throughout the winter months, though tactics change in that they do not eat so much, nor meander around all day. At that time of the year they will be found in deeper, warmer water, unless the venue has been cold for a number of weeks. Then the carp will sometimes seek the margins, especially if the sun has warmed the shallower water to any extent. All I can suggest is that the angler keep his binoculars focused, his eyes and ears open and try to find known winter venues (better advice still – save the urge until summer).

Those then, are the main items, necessities and basic information with which you may be welcomed into carping circles; it is a wonderful pastime, though with hidden dangers. I must say that it has become a cult, an addiction even, with a minority of brain-washed boneheads tuned to but one end – that of catching carp – to the exclusion of all other human traits or ambitions. You have been warned.

The foregoing has been an all too brief picture of this highly passionate world. I may be guilty of portraying a certain amount of cynicism, but I cannot help feeling that the ever-constant search for big carp has overtaken the magic, the very *essence* of it all. The tremendous excitement and the pleasure which the species can give has, to a certain extent, been sadly, and perhaps unknowingly, removed.

14 Perch

One of my fondest memories of a particular fish was not of my catching. One warm summer evening, fly fishing for trout from a boat on Westwood Lake in the company of a now departed friend, I was delighted for him when his rod arched over as a powerful fish took his large home-made colourful lure, aptly christened a Spectrum (I called it the Half-Parrot).

Minutes later, the most wonderfully coloured perch I have ever seen came to his net, a perch with the gold, green coat in full bloom, highlighted by the vertical black stripes, a proud, muscular form protected by the erect dorsal fin. In the glow of the evening sun that fish absolutely shone, and no camera could ever record the picture I have in my mind. Though

Travelling light for winter perch.

A deep snaggy hole in the Teme. The author took two 3lb perch from here in consecutive casts.

the rule was to retain all predatory coarse fish, there was no inclination in either of us to despatch it, so it returned to the reservoir intact. I cannot think of a more beautiful species in these isles.

Perch, in the manner of all other fish, eat everything from insects to their own offspring. The angler who wishes to catch big perch, however, can pin his hopes on but two main baits: worms and small fry.

It must be admitted that legering is perhaps not the best way to catch perch, although the method does have its good days. Even after considering the Walker/Arlesey Lake saga, where the great man invented his bomb to reach perch far out in deep water, to leger for perch can be counter-productive. Perch are carnivorous, much preferring to chase around after fry, especially when those fry are near the surface. As such, perch can be easily located, for they will herd the shoal of fry, surging into them to eat a few before moving out. When this happens, the fry spray to the surface, erupting in the urgency to escape; witness this phenomenon and you will have found perch. Fry-feeding apart, perch can be fairly easily located by searching out bankside features such as old sunken trees, overhanging bushes or, in the case of rivers, deeper slower holes near to the bank, for these are all places where fodder fry will congregate.

Pearl Lake abounds with decent perch. Along one bank is a swim predictably known as the perch hole. To the left is a large willow branch which sticks out over the lake, and under this branch, in less than two feet of

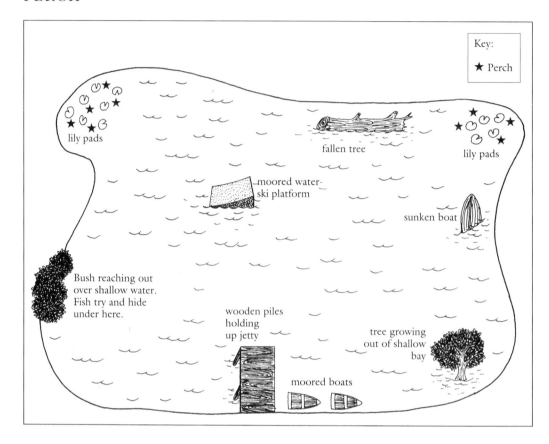

Key:
★ Perch

lily pads

fallen tree

lily pads

moored water-
ski platform

sunken boat

Bush reaching out
over shallow water.
Fish try and hide
under here.

wooden piles
holding
up jetty

tree growing
out of shallow
bay

moored boats

Fig. 23 Perch-holding features.

water, live perch, big ones, bigger than my best, which stands at a little over 3lb. Though the stocks have been sadly depleted, I am still hopeful enough to fish for them, using a simple ten-foot quiver-tip rod and line of 3.2lb direct to a size 10 hook. On to this goes one of the biggest, fattest, juiciest lobworms I can find from my wormery. The cast, because of the low branch, has to be skimmed across the surface, to be plopped into the swim directly under the lowest twigs. As the worm settles to the bottom, the point at which the line enters the water must be watched carefully, for a perch will drop a bait instantly should it sense resistance.

To take four or five fish above 2lb was not uncommon until the disaster in the hot summer of 1990 when the lake became dangerously low in oxygen. (The owner was quick in calling the assistance of the fire brigade who soon rigged up equipment to move 6,000 litres of water per minute, so oxygenating the lake to the degree where most of the fish were saved, though thousands of tiny perch perished. The lake overall is a much-improved fishery for that very reason.)

Predictably, I could never catch the really big perch during the caravanning season, which closes at the end of October. Previous to the loss of fish, I fished when I could into

The perch hole at Pearl Lake. Perch will always be attracted to snaggy swims.

This angry 1½ lb Pearl Lake perch took legered lobworm.

November, having great sport until the really hard frosts came along, after which catches deteriorated.

That 'perch hole' swim could be indicative of a perch area anywhere. If the fish are lethargic and need a little enticing, a twitched bait will sometimes produce a bite when nothing else will – much like bream. A normal take is a series of tugs, followed by a definite pull. Upon a confident bite, the line tightens across the surface as the fish moves off with the worm. A firm strike must now be made, for the mouth of a perch, as in all predators, is rather bony and it needs a firm strike to penetrate the membranes.

I have heard that perch are not classed as great fighters. I find this strange, for some of my most hair-raising tussles have been with perch, and none of them specimens. They are a species not given to tearing off to far regions, nor do they leap into the air as would an angry trout, but they are quite adept at tugging away like the blazes, twisting their heads from side to side in the effort to shake the hook. Also, the very fact that most good swims are in the vicinity of snags will make the smallest of perch head for them with renewed vigour, and make the angler aware of the need for caution – don't let them get too close.

The ethics of livebaiting are not for deliberation in this book. In my own opinion I can see no reason why a small fish should not be used to catch perch; if the angler did not use it, then there is a good chance a perch would eat it anyway. Legering with livebaits is difficult, at least in the basic context. It is far better to use a paternoster rig, where the bait is

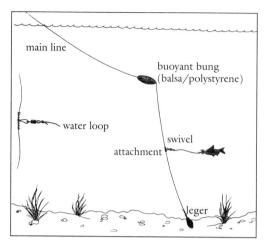

Fig. 24 Paternoster livebait suspended rig.

distance of the bank, a cast to the far side of the area will give enough leeway to move the leger gently towards the fishing position, recovering line a few inches at a time.

Perch fishing is a very uncomplicated branch of our sport. It is a roaming method where likely-looking spots must be sought out and which should be fished for only short periods, perhaps producing just one fish. There is no place for baskets or bivvies: a rod, reel, landing-net, plus a few bits of tackle around the pockets will suffice admirably.

This short chapter will, I hope, have given enough insight for the reader to generate a taste for perch fishing.

PROLOGUE

I have enjoyed writing this book. During the research I have re-lived old times, contacted old mates and made new friends. I believe also that I have become less idle, taking time to read the waters once again, to tie the correct knot to the correct length of leger-link; as a result, I'm catching more fish.

If, within the pages, some little method or idea will assist someone in catching an extra fish or two, then so be it, my job is done. But no matter how much a man may read of angling, he must still go out to do the business and catch his own fish; therein lies the crux of the matter. Above all, the best possible advice that I or any other author can give is priceless: no matter what branch of angling a man enters, be it sea, game, coarse, match or whatever, one thing must remain paramount: simply enjoy it.

suspended well off the bottom, lip-hooked and left to swim about within the confines of the hooklength. At times I like to use a sunken float which keeps the bait suspended off the bottom at whatever depth is set by the position of the hooklength attachment. With a 2–3in roach, a size 8 hook is quite big enough, pulled once through the top lip of the fish, and though perch have minute teeth, there is no need to opt for a wire trace. I have yet to lose a perch due to line chewing.

When paternostering, I like to use a leger which can be towed around a little by the livebait, so giving it just enough freedom to be almost natural. The take in this case leaves nothing to the imagination: the perch takes the bait, turns down and over goes the rod. This form of perch fishing is great fun, and if the shoal of fry can be located within casting

Index